The insiders' guide to recruiting & hiring hourly workers.

Shawn Boyer

FOUNDER & CEO of SNAGAJOB.COM

Editors: Mike Ward and Kyra Newman

Publisher: Heather Moose

Designer: Made Creative, Custom Built Brands

Printer: WebbMason

Job well done.

As with anything worth doing, this book has been a true team effort. Mike Ward and Kyra Newman, the two editors of this book, have worked tirelessly and wonderfully together to turn a concept into reality. Thank you both for your passion and dedication, from research to interviews, to writing and editing. You have been fantastic, and I am very appreciative.

Thank you to Heather Moose, our publisher, for pushing us constantly with deadlines and holding us all accountable.

Thank you to all of the people at SnagAJob.com for making this one of the best places in the world to work—I'm the most blessed guy around to be able to work with such incredible people.

Thank you to our clients—both employers and job seekers. To our employers, thank you for partnering with us and allowing us to serve you and to glean best practices from you, the best-run companies in the world. It's an honor to work with you. And, to our job seekers, you are the backbone of this great country, and we hope to continue to honor you with everything that we do. Thank you for all of your incredibly hard work—24 hours a day, 7 days a week, 365 days a year— that makes the real economic engine of this country work.

And, of course, thank you to my wonderful wife Tennille for being supportive (and a critic when needed!) of the writing of this book and to our daughter Macy, who makes every day just a ton of fun.

-Shawn

Contents

SECTION 2: METRICS & TACTICS

Introduction

So, why take any of your valuable time to read this book? There are thousands of books on recruiting and selection, etc. But you will not find many that focus specifically on hourly recruitment. And you'll find even fewer that lay out some simple steps to help your company gain a competitive advantage over your competitors. So, why is hourly recruitment important?

In our research, we have found that companies that really put a premium on the recruitment of their front-line hourly employees have better top-line and bottom-line performance than the rest of the pack.

For a compelling example of what a huge financial impact focusing on hourly workers can have on your company, consider Starbucks for just a minute. In "Pour Your Heart into It" by Howard Schultz, Chairman and CEO of Starbucks, he cites the following incredible numbers. Most retailers and fast-food chains have a turnover rate ranging from 150 percent to as high as 400 percent a year for their hourly employees. At Starbucks, turnover for their hourly employees (their baristas) is 60–65 percent. With 80 percent+ of their 170,000 employees being hourly and the cost to train a new hire being approximately $3,000, that's an incredible $459 million savings each year.

The bottom line? It's that there is a direct correlation between a company's financial performance and the recruitment of their front-line hourly employees. That's a pretty compelling story. And, it's not an overly complicated one. We hope to lay out for you the essential ingredients in this book so that you can incorporate them into your organization and be able to benefit from the fruits of those efforts just as some of the world's most elite organizations have done.

So what are the commonalities of these companies that have demonstrated this advantage?

1. Value the individual

They put a very high premium on their hourly employees and value the individual—
really value them—no matter their position within the organization.

2. Hourly recruitment is critical

As an organization, they decided that hourly recruitment is critical to their success,
and they established clear objectives.

3. Develop a strategy

They developed a concise strategy for hourly recruitment to reach those objectives.

4. Develop tactics and measure them

They developed the tactics to support the strategy and measured themselves
constantly as to how they were doing against their objectives.

CHAPTER 1

All for One. One for All.

Value the individual—and watch employee loyalty do the heavy lifting for your recruitment brand.

There are many differences between salary workers and hourly workers—turnover rate, socioeconomic status, where they work, where they live, jobs that they perform, where they spend their free time, how they spend their money, etc. But one thing is a constant—whether it's the CEO or the janitor, all workers must know and really feel that they are valued as individuals within your organization and that what they do every day matters. Former Citibank CEO Walter Shipley says, "Everyone feels that he or she makes a difference to the success of the organization. When that happens, people feel centered and that gives their work meaning."

Every great organization gets that. And they make purposeful efforts to ensure that everyone within the organization knows.

In most organizations, the customer experience is vital—we would probably all agree that this is a no-brainer. So what happens if your customer has a bad encounter? What are the repercussions of that? Do they never come back? Do they tell all of their friends and co-workers how bad it was and to not frequent your business?

And whose job is it to ensure that your customers have a great experience? In most instances, this lifeblood of your company rests with the 18-year-old high school senior who works 20 hours a week for your company. Can you afford for her not to know how much she is valued by your organization and how critically important her job is to the success of the company? "If you treat your employees as interchangeable cogs in a wheel, they will view you with the same affection," Schultz says.[1]

Below are two examples of companies who are renowned for both their financial success and their commitment to their hourly employees. Our contention is that there is a direct correlation between the two.

First, Starbucks. We mentioned them in the introduction, and we'll mention them again in later chapters. Why? Because they check both boxes squarely—great financial success as a company and passion about treating their hourly employees as partners (and truly partners).

Inspired leadership should be felt from the perches of the corporate offices to the front-line registers—and should be embodied by every employee.

The number one investment companies can make is in their people, as loyalty reaps a consistent domino effect of rewards.

> "Good leaders make people feel they're at the very heart of things, not at the periphery."
>
> – Warren Bennis, "The Maxwell Daily Reader", John Maxwell[II]

Since the original Starbucks location opened in 1984, the company has grown to over 16,000 stores worldwide in 2008.

At the heart of that success, is their people. According to Howard Schultz, "From the beginning, I wanted employees to identify with the mission of the company and to have the sense of accomplishment that goes with being part of a successful team. That meant defining a strong sense of purpose and listening to input from people at all levels of the enterprise..." In the Starbucks mission statement, which was crafted by people from all levels within the organization (and most definitely by their hourly employees), the first guiding principle is "Provide a great work environment and treat each other with respect and dignity." They have backed that up with action. Below are just a few of the things they've done to underscore that they truly do value each employee:

1. **Full health benefits**
2. **Mission review** — Starbucks has set up a mission review system so that any employee who thinks a decision made within the organization is counter to the mission statement can submit a card indicating that. It will be responded to by the leadership of the company within two weeks.
3. **Stock option plan** — Employees get "Bean Stock" options—up to 14 percent of gross pay, plus the option of buying additional shares at a steep discount.

Howard Schultz also noted that "Ultimately, Starbucks can't flourish and win customers' hearts without the passionate devotion of our employees. In business, that passion comes from ownership, trust and loyalty. If you undermine any of those, employees will view their work as just another job. Sometimes we lose sight of that at Starbucks, especially as we get larger and a distance develops between me and the newest hire in the newest store. But I know, in my heart, if we treat people as a line item under expenses, we're not living up to our goals and our values. Their passion and devotion is our number-one competitive advantage. Lose it, and we've lost the game."[III]

Our second example is, Chick-fil-A. They have grown from one restaurant in 1946 to more than 1,400 restaurants in 2009, with 40 consecutive years of positive sales growth. In 2006, they reached the $2 billion mark in revenue, taking only 6 years to go from $1 billion to $2 billion. The chain produced more than $2.6 billion in revenue in 2007, up 16 percent from the prior year.

Fil-A'ing the competition

Source	Customer service ranking
2007 ▶ QSR Magazine	**1st** in drive-thru accuracy, menu board appearance and employee smiles
2007 ▶ Zagats & "TODAY"	**1st** in fast food industry
2008 ▶ JD Powers & Business Week	**22nd** overall in the nation

To what does Chick-fil-A attribute so much success with such a simple concept? Their people. At the heart of it, it is Chick-fil-A's maniacal commitment to their people— every single person within their organization.

In Chick-fil-A's annual message, they say, "At Chick-fil-A, our people are much more than a commodity or a number to be counted. At Chick-fil-A, we count years of service and smiles on the faces of our franchised Operators, their team members and our corporate office staff."

Fred Reichheld, author of *The Loyalty Effect* and *Loyalty Rules!,* says, "Founder Truett Cathy has so effectively marshaled the loyalty effect economics that he can afford to... grow the chain and to contribute approximately 10 percent of profits to charity. This loyalty effect, the full range of economic and human benefits that accrue to leaders who treat their customers, operators, and employees in a manner worthy of their loyalty, is at the core of most of the truly successful growth companies in the world today. And there is no clearer case study of the loyalty effect than Chick-fil-A."[IV]

Sources

I   Schultz, Howard. *Pour Your Heart Into It: How Starbucks Built a Company One Cup at a Time.* Hyperion Books. 1997: 138.

II   Maxwell, John. *The Maxwell Daily Reader*. Nelson Bibles. 2001: 14.

III   Schultz, Howard. *Pour Your Heart Into It: How Starbucks Built a Company One Cup at a Time.* Hyperion Books. 1997: 138.

IV   Reichheld, Fred, Author of *The Loyalty Effect* and *Loyalty Rules!*

Notes

CHAPTER 2

Setting Hire Goals

Learn how turnover and cost-per-hire buoy and craft your hourly recruitment objectives.

Establish objectives: First, nail down your fundamental objectives of hourly recruitment.
What is it that you want to accomplish that will make a meaningful difference within your organization? Are you trying to reduce turnover? Increase sales per employee? Reduce your cost per hire? All of the above?

Organizational buy-in: Build your case internally.
Before you start down a path within your department of trying to effectuate any radical changes, you first need to have complete organizational buy-in. Otherwise, you're not going to get the resources (financial or otherwise) you need to maximize your opportunity.
So how do you do that?

Prove it will make a difference—with data.
We'll talk more about key measurements in Chapter 3. But to get the solid backing that you need internally, you must demonstrate with data how achieving those objectives will make a meaningful financial difference to your organization.

Turnover and cost-per-hire are the cornerstone statistics of your hourly recruitment goals and strategy.

Honing in on hard numbers is vital to selling your recruitment story to key decision makers.

"If you aim at nothing, you'll hit it every time."

– B. J. Marshall

For example, if your organization currently has turnover of 100 percent, and the cost-per-hire is $1,000 and you hire 1,000 people a year, what would the financial impact to the company be if you could just move the turnover needle by 10 percent? (Figure 1) It's $100,000 per year, and over a three-year period that's $300,000. And if your organization is growing 5 percent per year (including new units), that takes your savings to over $100,000 per year and more than $315,000 over a three-year period.

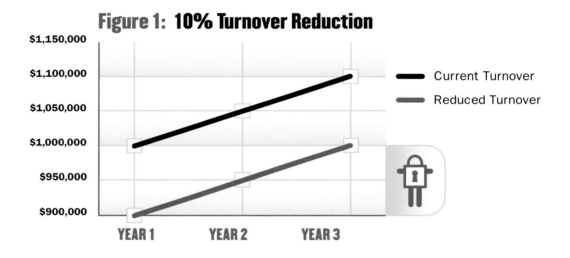

Figure 1: 10% Turnover Reduction

Now, what if you also were able to reduce the cost-per-hire by 10 percent to $900/hire? (Figure 2) In the first year, you save an additional $100,000, and over the same three-year period you save over $315,000 (assuming same growth rates).

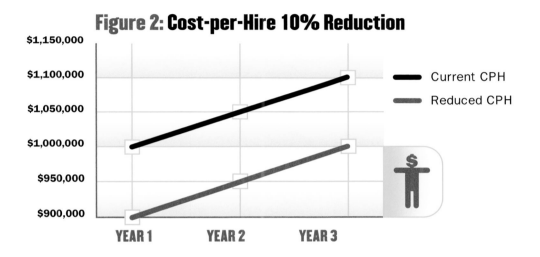

Figure 2: Cost-per-Hire 10% Reduction

— Current CPH
— Reduced CPH

Let's say that because you're hiring better-fit employees within your organization that you could expect a .5 percent increase in sales per full-time employee. (Figure 3) If your organization has $100 million in sales, then that's a $500,000 improvement to the top line each year. And when you take into account the compounding effect, this improvement yields $3.5 million over a three-year period.

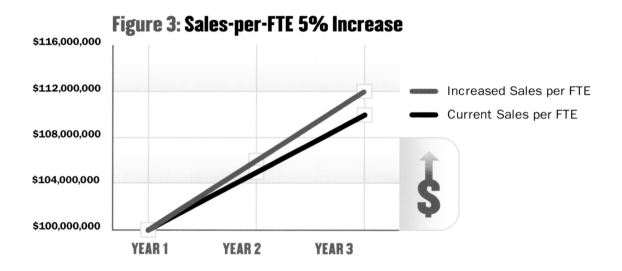

Figure 3: Sales-per-FTE 5% Increase

Obviously, this could be a very compelling case to take to the senior leadership of your organization—assuming the resources needed to obtain these objectives makes financial sense, which we'll talk about more later. The important thing here, regardless of what objectives you have or what assumptions you use, is that you can clearly demonstrate that your objectives have a direct positive financial impact on the company. If you do that, you'll significantly increase your chances of getting the corporate buy-in you need in order to get the resources required to meet your objectives.

THE BOTTOM LINE

When you combine the impact of the three objectives over the course of three years, it plays out as follows:

**Three-Year Cumulative
Bottom-Line Improvement:**

$3,845,158

$2,500,000	
$2,000,000	
$1,500,000	
$1,000,000	
$500,000	
$0	

YEAR 1

YEAR 2

YEAR 3

Understand your objectives.

Take a moment to break down your organization's current turnover and cost-per-hire against your dream scenario. First, fill in the appropriate fields in the left-hand column. Then indicate where you would like to take these metrics to, expressed as a percentage. Finally, calculate what improving these key business metrics can bring to your bottom line.

	Current Numbers	% Improvement Goal	Numbers After Achieved Goal
Total Hourly Employees			
Turnover			
Cost-per-Hire			
Total Recruitment Spend:	$	Savings:	$

What are your company's top three hourly recruitment objectives?

☑ **We must...**

☑ **We should...**

☑ **We have to...**

Notes

Call a timeout, gather your team together and draw up a strategic game plan to learn who you really are.

**QUICK READ**

Call a timeout before you get started to craft a winning game plan.

The game plan shapes and informs your tactics and playbook.

Become self-aware before you decide who you want to be. You may be further—or closer —than you think.

As with any objectives, they're useless unless you have the strategy (we'll refer to it as the "game plan") in place in order to meet those objectives. Below are some of the questions that need to be answered in order to create a highly effective hourly recruitment strategy.

1. Who are you as an organization?

Obviously, your organization has defined this from a customer brand perspective, but it also has to do that from a recruitment brand perspective. Hopefully, the two mirror each other.

Companies that really "get it" know who they are and we all know them, as well. Take UPS, whose "What can BROWN do for you?" motto is a challenge posed to potential customers and employees. Both audiences are promised world-class reliability—and UPS delivers steadfastly times two. From on-time, accurate package delivery for customers to competitive tuition assistance and discount programs for employees, these consistent benefits are expectations UPS always meets.

Building on its leading consumer brand, Seattle-based coffee retailer Starbucks has strategically built a well-respected employment brand, integrated across multiple channels, that reinforces its respect for its people – known internally as "partners." Partners predominantly comprise hourly workers in the chain's company-operated stores. Founded in 1971, Starbucks repeatedly generates national accolades as a great place to work, boasting benefits such as medical and stock options for eligible part-time hourly workers. Those investments result in partners' longevity with and goodwill toward the company, which spreads to customers in the marketplace. In turn, these customers are potential new hourly employees.

"Our business is big on the investment we make in the people who are our partners," said Phil Hendrickson, manager of global talent sourcing for Starbucks. "There's something enduring about the Starbucks benefits and the Starbucks culture that touches people in the retail industry. The investment pays off. At the end of the day, it does work."

A quick check to see if you and your organization really get this: Can you write a one-sentence purpose statement as an employer?

2. Who do you want on your team?

Once you know who you are as an employer, it makes it a lot easier to know who you want on your team! Not that anyone wants someone who moves at a slug's pace, but is the need for an employee to move and act quickly imperative to your company? Or is it most important that they are super extroverted with a love of interacting with people all day long? Or is it more important for them to be as sweet as Aunt Bee? Is a love of electronics important? Or do you need leaders (demonstrated through community activities, school, sports, etc.)? Do you want some combination of these traits?

Disney has a winning game plan that makes its employees—called "cast members"—true ambassadors of its customer-facing brand. Its three-pronged approach to finding five-star employees focuses on candidates' *availability* (on weekends and during prime vacation times), *appearance* (consistent with the Disney brand) and *attitude* (you're always "on stage").

We know to some degree that it depends on the position, but we would argue that your organization should be able to articulate the most important attributes it is looking for in an employee in a couple of sentences or less. At SnagAJob.com, we look for 3 simple (but not so easy to find) qualities: smart, hungry and humble. Can you describe in one sentence who you want on your team?

3. Where do you find them?

We'll talk a lot more about this in Chapter 5, but to some degree where you find your people depends on who you're trying to find. You need to do the research to figure out where you'll reach your future employee audience. Is it your customers? The Container Store, which also is consistently ranked as one of FORTUNE's "100 Best Companies to Work For", recruits directly from its customer base, an amazing luxury when your consumer brand and employment brand intersect. If you're a high-end steak and lobster restaurant, then probably not. If you're a quick casual restaurant or convenience store, then possibly yes. Do your potential employees read the paper? Are they online? If so, where?

This sounds basic, but connecting the dots is essential. Do the research to figure out where your best hourly employees are spending their time and searching for employment.

4. How do you get them to love it at your company?

Simple—make the environment match what you held out to them in the recruitment process. Chances are, they took the job because they thought they would enjoy working with your organization—prove to them that they were right!

One thing that we've seen time and again is that the best companies practice what they preach in the recruitment process. What you see is what you get, and then some. If you pride yourself in being customer-focused, then pride yourself in treating your employees as customers. And customers are not expendable.

Consider what Schultz says: "It is an ironic fact that, while retail and restaurant businesses live or die on customer service, their employees have among the lowest pay and worst benefits of any industry. These people are not only the heart and soul but also the public face of the company. Every dollar earned passes through their hands. In a store or restaurant, the customer's experience is vital: One bad encounter, and you've lost a customer for life."[1]

If you've preached that you're a fast-moving, hard-hitting company, then don't put handcuffs on your new employees. Or at least just put training wheels on them and take them off as quickly as you can! The takeaway is: Be who you say you are.

5. What tactics do you have in place to support your game plan?

Just as you need the strategy to reach your objectives, you need simple, repeatable tactics to support your game plan. We'll spend the balance of this book talking about the tactics needed to support your hourly recruitment strategy—whatever that may be!

Do your brands mirror each other?

Do your customer brand and employer brand match up? It's important that while they make separate appeals to their target audiences, there is still solid overlap and consistency in their messages. To find out if your customer and employer brands intersect, write each down in the space provided. If they don't overlap, revise one of the two to forge greater consistency.

Customer Brand:

Employer Brand:

Revised Customer or Employer Brand:

Sources

I   Schultz, Howard. *Pour Your Heart Into It: How Starbucks Built a Company One Cup at a Time.* Hyperion Books.
1997: 125.

Notes

CHAPTER 4

Measuring Up

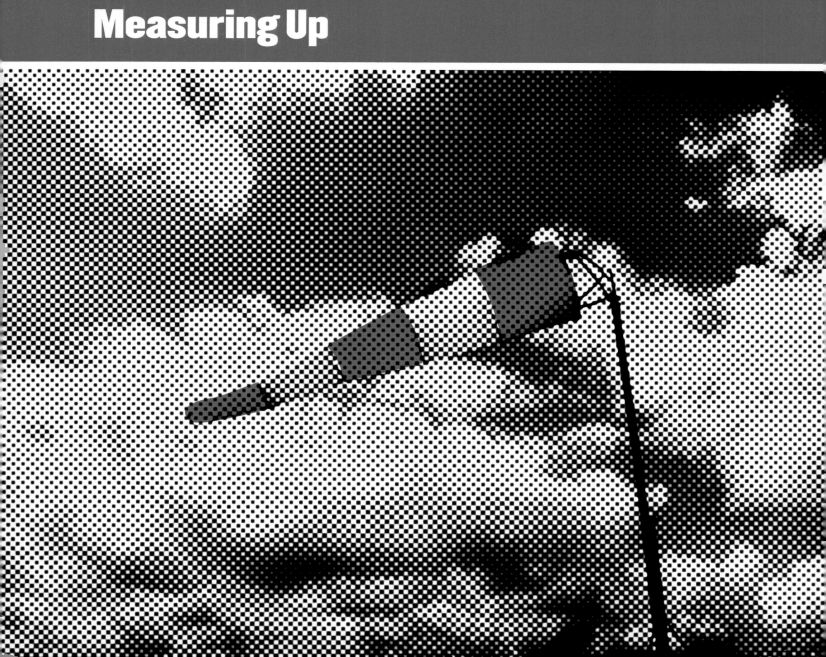

Set up key measurements to track your own success—and to find out where you stack up among the competition.

"If you don't measure something, you can't change it. The process of leadership is one of painting a vision, then saying how you're going to get there, and then measuring whether you're actually getting there. Otherwise, you risk only talking about great things but not accomplishing them," says former Massachusetts Governer, Mitt Romney.

So you've outlined your objectives and your game plan. What next? How do you know whether you're making progress towards hitting your objectives? Further to the point, how do you know where you currently are so that you know how much progress you need to make? If your objectives aren't quantifiable, then they are ultimately hollow.

Best-of-breed organizations measure almost everything—and certainly that includes recruitment. John Chambers, CEO of Cisco, often states that Cisco can measure anything at any time. Jeff Bezos, CEO of Amazon, is known to stop a meeting as soon as it's underway if there's no data to support or refute the issues being discussed.

 **QUICK READ**

If you don't know how to measure your success, then you're already failing.

Before you pull out your ruler, scale and measuring cup, hone in on the key metrics that drive your success—and determine how and how often you'll capture these key measurments.

So, what are the metrics that you should be tracking? First, you need to identify the ones that matter the most to achieving your objectives, so you'll have to go back to Chapter 2 to determine those. And, in our opinion, if the following don't fall within that set of metrics, then you need to add them.

- **Time to fill**
- **Cost-per-hire**
- **Turnover (both voluntary and involuntary)**
- **Sales/FTE**

Note: We will talk in much more detail in Chapter 9 about the various systems available to help you track these important metrics.

None of what we describe here is rocket science—you'll find it in virtually every MBA textbook. However, there are numerous companies who don't do this (or don't do this well) because they don't get accurate data or timely data or any data at all. We've found that the best companies are maniacal about their people metrics and make it a priority.

"No score, no game."

– Ken Blanchard,
Gung Ho[1]

MEASURE TWICE. HIRE ONCE.

To measure your hourly recruitment performance, you'll need several basics in place. The keys to this are establishing the following:

1. The metrics you will track
Which ones are the most important?

2. Your baseline performance against those metrics
Where are you now?

3. Your target performance against those metrics
Where do you want to go?

4. Incremental milestones
How do you know if you're making progress towards your ultimate objectives?

5. The frequency with which you measure
How frequently do you need to check in to ensure you're making progress and to make tweaks along the way?

6. The tools that will allow you to measure
What systems do you need to help you measure those metrics easily so that you can obtain the data with the frequency that you need?

Calculate metrics that matter to you:

Metric	Data points to consider	Determine your actual metric
Cost-per-hire	■ Overall recruitment costs ■ Number of hires ■ Training costs ■ Onboarding and time-to-productivity estimates Notes: Be sure to align your timeline for costs and hires; the more you can break down your data to reflect designated hiring, the more valuable your responses about hourly hiring.	
Retention	■ Hire date ■ Exit date ■ Designated window	
Other metrics:	■ ■ ●	

Elevate the weakest link in the metric chain.

The following have been identified as key metrics for many businesses. Rank them in order, from 1 to 4, with "1" being the metric that's most relevant in determining your own organization's success.

	Time to fill		Cost-per-hire		Turnover		Sales/full-time employee

Now focus on the metric you labeled as least relevant to your business. Odds are, this is also the metric receiving the least amount of attention from your HR team. Let's change that right now. Brainstorm below three ways you can improve this metric.

1.

2.

3.

Sources

I   Blanchard, Ken and Bowles, Sheldon. *Gung Ho! Turn on the People in Any Organization*. Harper Collins: 1998: page 137.

Increase the top of your funnel.

From a practical perspective, the more people you put into the top of the funnel, the better chance you have of getting the right number of people coming out of the bottom of your funnel. Thus, one of the tactics you need to have in place is a mechanism to increase your flow of candidates.

In the following chapter, we'll talk about two ways to widen this metaphorical applicant funnel: determining the best online source for your best new employees, and creating compelling job descriptions as recruitment firepower.

 ## Ask your employees. Who would you hire?

If you have created an environment in which people love your organization, your people will refer their friends and colleagues who they think will be a great fit for the organization. And the nice thing about that is that your organization is getting a known commodity—or at least more known than if no one knows the individual.

There are a couple of strategies to help your efforts with referrals:

Communicate your openings to your existing employee base

Too many times there are openings within the organization at the unit level and the current employees are not made aware of it. Develop a trigger so that each time a job is open, you communicate that to the team. And, if you are always in hiring mode, make sure you let all of your team know that! Send out monthly reminders that you are hiring—keep it fresh.

 **QUICK READ**

The Internet delivers better candidates for you in ways that are quicker and cheaper for your business.

Online recruitment comes in different flavors; you need to pick the tactics that deliver the right candidates for you.

Sell the total package—not just titles and wages.

Be ready to talk with candidates the moment your job posting goes online.

Give them monetary incentives to refer people to the organization

While a lot of people will refer others in the organization simply because they love it, you certainly can increase your chances of referrals by paying a monetary incentive. And make the amount substantial enough to be worthwhile. Obviously, you want to structure the incentives so that they're only payable after the new hire has been with you for some minimum period of time. The monetary reward will do two things: get people to think about referrals more often, and show how committed your organization is to getting the right people.

After a referral is hired, make sure you tell everyone who referred the individual. Once it comes time to pay the award, gather everyone around and give the award for all to see. That keeps the incentives fresh in people's minds and it shows that employees really are reaping the benefits of the referral system.

A successful referral system also needs one more rule: The worker who referred a new employee needs to serve as his or her mentor throughout the first 30 days of employment.

Sources of External Hire

Tactics	Percentage
Referrals	28.2%
Job Boards	25.7%
Other	12.5%
Direct Sourcing	9.4%
Boomerangs (Rehires)	4.8%
Print Ads	4.6%
Colleges	3.8%
Agencies	3.3%
Temp-to-Hires	3.0%
Career Fairs	2.3%
Search Engine	1.2%
Walk-ins	0.8%
Open Houses	0.7%

– CareerXRoads

The web can energize the power of your job postings from static cling to a surging electric charge.

More than ever, people of all ages are going online as part of their job search. Other than employee referrals, no other strategy generates the numbers of hires attributed to job boards. In 2007, recruiters reported that nearly a third of new hires were sourced online.[I] And the fastest growing segment of those with access to online job postings hails from low-income households,[II] or in other words, those right in the hourly job seeker demographic. Put simply, the Internet can deliver:

More candidates: The number of job seekers applying for positions online grows every day.

Better candidates: Screening questions and assessment tools help you focus immediately on job seekers who are the right fit for your business.

Cheaper acquisition: Online recruiting rates are more cost-effective than traditional newspaper and other advertising tactics, driving a healthier bottom line for your business.

Faster turnaround: Technology delivers automation, which can allow you to quickly post and fill jobs online. There's no need to miss top talent while you're waiting for your newspaper ad to be printed next week.

With an industry standard turnover rate of more than 100 percent for hourly workers, American businesses are having to reload their hourly positions more than once a year with fresh faces from the 80-million-strong hourly workforce. And both recruiters and job seekers have found that going online is the best way to keep up with this vigorous pace. People most frequently found their last job through an ad posted on an online job board, reports WEDDLE's 2008 Source of Employment Survey.[III] Making the right hiring choice is not inexpensive. In fact, a report from Saratoga, a division of PricewaterhouseCoopers, shows that the average cost-per-hire for an hourly worker is $989.[IV] This bottom-line impact needs further definition: **Hiring candidates through online methods can be 10 times cheaper than hiring them through traditional advertising channels.**[V]

The recruitment industry has taken notice. In fact, according to a 2007 study by Borrell Associates, recruiting became "the first major advertising category to slip from the iron grasp of traditional media and become 'majority controlled' by online."[VI] In its 2008 report, Borrell Associates projects 43.5 percent growth in online recruitment spending over the next four years.[VII] That growth, along with significant investments in full-service recruiting firms, comes as baby boomers begin to retire. A smaller generation is following them, and the young Generation Y is still inexperienced in the marketplace, according to Peter Conti Jr., senior vice president with Borrell Associates. "What we're going to see is a scramble to fill these positions," he adds.

The Internet has earned its position as one of the best channels to reach out to a large volume of hourly job seekers. The challenge for online recruitment, however, is to increase its sophistication to better match qualified candidates to the jobs that are out there, Conti says. The better that job boards can align their postings with the job seekers who access them, the better the results. Niche boards link job seekers with open jobs by type, industry or other demographic, such as minority group. For example, ChicagoJobs.com promotes jobs in the Chicago market, BigTruckDrivingJobs.com offers trucking gigs, Dice.com provides technology jobs and SnagAJob.com serves up hourly employment opportunities.

"We see great opportunities for the niche boards. These are becoming highly targeted places to find highly targeted workers. It's a perfect fit. We think this is still only the beginning," says Conti, who expects a significant growth spurt starting in 2011. "As the awareness factor increases, there is still a lot of growth to come for online recruitment." The number of job opportunities available online continues to grow. WEDDLE's today acknowledges more than 50,000 U.S. job boards and career portals, representing a 25 percent gain in just five years.[VIII] The downside, WEDDLE's observes, is that many recruiters limit their use to a handful of familiar sites rather than strategically advertising their jobs on boards that might better deliver the right talent.

"It's a break-out for anyone in the recruiting industry if they can produce a product that can lighten the load for a recruiter," Conti says. "Recruiters are going to use a variety of sources. They are going to be looking at a number of places to be successful."

WHO'S ONLINE?

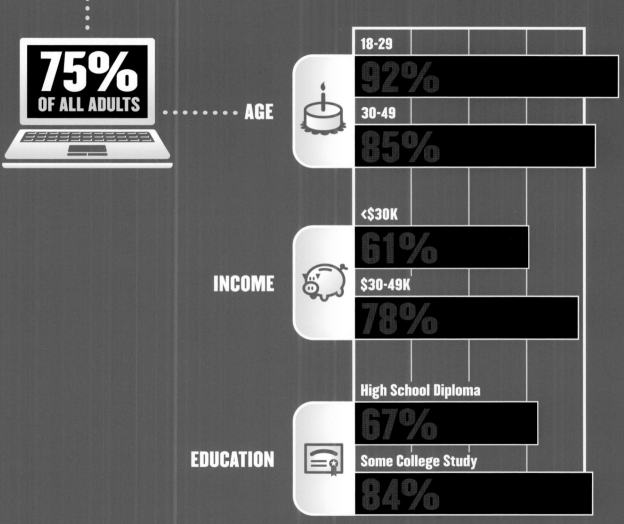

75% OF ALL ADULTS

AGE

18-29
92%

30-49
85%

INCOME

<$30K
61%

$30-49K
78%

EDUCATION

High School Diploma
67%

Some College Study
84%

– *Pew Internet & American Life Project* [IX]

How to maximize your company site for hourly job seekers ▮

Separate hourly and salaried jobs: Create defined and intuitive paths for hourly job seekers to find the right-fit jobs.

List hourly jobs by location: Hourly job seekers want to work close to where they live, preferably within 10 miles. You might even consider incorporating mapping functionality.

Allow seekers to apply immediately: Job seekers are interested in working for you at that precise moment they're on your site, so capture them on the spot with an online application process.

Don't require a resumé: Hourly candidates have job experience, but they may not have a resumé or know how to produce one. Give them an opportunity to tell you about their background and why they're the right fit for your jobs by completing a simple online Q&A that builds a job profile.

Legal ease: While you want to guarantee your application meets all legal requirements, make sure this is a quick and easy process. You don't want to complicate the application process with unnecessary hurdles.

Push out the applications: Often, the hourly hiring process is decentralized, so make sure your technology pushes quality applicants directly to your hiring managers—don't rely on them to go looking. The quicker you get top talent to them, the quicker they can hire the people they need. (And don't forget to tell applicants that you've received their applications, either through a real-time online submission cue or an email. This will help stymie their fears of sending applications into a "black hole" void.)

Learn more about Talent Management Systems in Chapter 6, Screening for Right-Fit Hires. Topics include:
- Applicant tracking
- Online applications
- Online assessments

Screen your candidates: Worried about getting too many online applications to review? Incorporate screening tools, such as assessment questions, that draw out top job seekers who meet your requirements.

Track your candidates: Make sure you have a way to follow applicants through the hiring stage, whether it's with a Talent Management System or another tool.

Weigh your online recruitment options before scaling up.

Job seekers today have a growing range of online resources for finding jobs. By better understanding the different ways that job seekers can find your jobs, you can focus on the approach that works best for your needs—or even better, find benefits in tapping into a blend of services.

Your Company Website

If your business has a website, you should have a method for connecting visitors with your hourly jobs. While a smaller business may find a phone number sufficient when hiring volumes are low, you'll probably want to invest in automated tools, such as an Applicant Management System or a Talent Management System (TMS), as your workforce needs escalate. A TMS can manage higher numbers of applicants and get the qualified candidates efficiently to your hiring managers, but you need to find a system that is specifically designed and built to support your hourly candidate strategy and process—including targeted workforce assessments. A TMS allows you to then track your hires over their lifecycles with your business, letting you capture information about your best workers that you can leverage when finding your next new hires. Recruiting through your own business website is free, and you market your jobs when you market your company.

Hourly Recruitment Tactics

Medium	Advantages	Disadvantages
Classified ads	▪ Traditional way that people have looked for hourly jobs ▪ Community papers connect you to local workforce	▪ Require costly investment for limited amount of information ▪ Visibility may be restricted to date of publication ▪ Hard to track ▪ If hiring in multiple markets, you need to pay for multiple newspapers and don't have a central location for managing
"Help Wanted" signs	▪ Captures interest of people who know your business and live in the area	▪ Limit applicant pool to only those who see your sign
Referrals	▪ Identify potential candidates who are the right fit for your organization ▪ Build morale by paying referral bonuses	▪ Create potential morale issues if employees don't understand why you don't hire people they recommend
Job fairs	▪ Brings together a volume of job seekers, often related by industry ▪ Allow you to interview and hire on the spot	▪ Limited access and time window
Company website	▪ Job seekers who know your brand will be able to find your jobs online with relative ease ▪ Free!	▪ Seekers may not know to go directly to your site for job postings
General job boards	▪ Connect you immediately with large pool of applicants ▪ Results can be measured	▪ May not attract the specific job seeker profile you're looking for
Niche specialized boards	▪ Deliver more highly targeted candidates so you spend less time screening qualified applicants ▪ Growing in popularity as seekers gain awareness of job websites catering specifically to their needs	▪ Have a less-recognized brand among general job seekers because of specialized focus

– SnagAJob.com [x]

General Job Boards

These include such sites as Monster.com, CareerBuilder.com and HotJobs.com. General job boards attract significant traffic and help you build your application volume. They have measured performance and may offer sophisticated technology, along with partnerships with other online media, such as newspapers, which extend a posting's visibility. With a greater focus on salaried jobs, however, the general job boards carry fees that can outstrip your hourly recruitment budget, and untargeted job postings may generate a lower quality applicant for your hourly positions. Heavy volumes of job listings also mean that your postings may quickly drop to a seeker's second or third page of local results. This is a problem for hourly worker-fueled businesses that never stop recruiting.

Niche Job Boards

These sites are focused on specific industries or categories, and deliver a higher quality of applicants unique to those boards. We consider our company, SnagAJob.com, to be a niche site, as we specifically match hourly job seekers with hourly jobs. Other niche sites focus on job openings in targeted industries, such as healthcare or hospitality, and Borrell Associates projects the biggest growth to occur within these specialty boards. The benefits extend to the technology and user interface, which are tailored for both the employer and job seeker experience, and generally higher levels of customer service, customization and flexibility. Some niche sites are continuing to build their brand recognition, which may make it challenging for you to justify your initial spend to your management team. However, you'll also find that your cost to post to these niche boards is more closely aligned with the pay for those positions.

Social Networking Sites

These include MySpace, Facebook and a slew of others. While only a fraction of users currently are posting their resumés on social networking sites—specifically, 24 percent of users 18 to 29 years old [XI]—don't discount the influence these popular sites have on your hiring practices. Most major job boards already partner with popular social networking sites to drive application volume, and their impact is expected to only intensify.

You may find that you already have a faithful following on a social networking site that evolved from employees' grassroots efforts. Whether that has occurred or not, you might consider building a fresh company profile, which allows you to describe your business and culture. Depending on the social networking website and the functionality offered, these profiles can include everything from discussion boards and photo threads to blogs and real-time chats. But before you start brainstorming and embarking on this cutting-edge tactic, here are a few best practices to consider:

Plan: Decide what filters, if any, you'll place on content. Does user-generated content need to be reviewed before it's published? If so, how long should users expect to wait to see their content live after submitting? And who's reviewing this content? Will profanity or negative comments be filtered? Be cautious about filtering feedback too much because you want to present your company as authentic and credible. Strike a balance that shows you're candid with users and still respectful of company stakeholders.

Recruit: Select a few responsible employees to make postings regularly about the benefits of working there, as well as the latest company news. All company employees should be honest in always identifying themselves as such to encourage open and honest dialogue. Transparency is key. You don't want to get busted posing as someone you're not.

Promote: Make sure your potential candidates, new hires and existing workers know they have an online community on which to collaborate.

Engage: Ask your workers questions. Answer employee comments. And counter misinformation about company matters as accurately—and professionally—as possible.

Social networking is a fast-growing hourly recruitment strategy that, if executed and maintained responsibly, can really help you establish credibility with the online audience, especially teens and 20-somethings. Follow the tips, and it could become a windfall of top-notch hourly workers.

Learn more about social networking in Chapter 9, Taking It to the Next Level.

Social media connects younger workers.

Social networking sites are increasingly creating ways to engage today's newest workers. Nation's Restaurant News notes that "interactive sites, unlike e-mail or newsletters, can engage workers, particularly younger employees who've grown up using the Internet and enjoy bonding with peers online."[XII]

For example, McDonald's built StationM.com to create an online gathering spot for its 650,000 employees in the United States and Canada. The company aimed to give its employees a way to discuss topics and issues that are relevant to them.

Private sites encourage participation among workers who may be hesitant to join a public discussion. They also generate direct communication with front-line workers who traditionally are at the end of message trails within a major organization. One negative aspect of these private sites is that if they're also meant for recruitment purposes, they face an uphill road in building awareness. But you can still leverage the power of these sites by promoting them to job applicants as part of your corporate culture.

Vertical search engines/job aggregators

Sites such as Indeed.com and SimplyHired.com, which are surging in popularity, function similarly to Google in that they're search engines, only dedicated to job postings. These vertical search engines are constantly scouring company sites, online classified newspaper ads and the major job boards to find and compile job postings. You can also opt to provide a feed of your jobs to these sites; however, you generally cannot post directly to job aggregators. Job seekers who use these sites will see job titles and a brief description of your jobs, but when they click the links to learn more, they'll be brought to the site from which the postings originate.

Additional downsides to vertical search engines include the fact that your jobs may be cross-posted well after they've been filled, and the fact that seekers cannot apply to your jobs directly through these sites. You also have no control over how vertical search engines are presenting and promoting your jobs, leaving your brand exposed.

78%
of job seekers
**are using the Internet
as a key part of their
job search.**

– U.S. Conference Board, 2007

Integrating online job postings into your recruitment strategy doesn't require you to upgrade your personal technology skills. The job boards, search engines and even your corporate webmaster have the IT know-how and resources that take care of behind-the-scenes coding and systems operations. The only thing you need to do is determine your goals for online hourly recruiting and to identify the current tactics that can deliver those targeted results. You focus on recruiting; your online partner focuses on the technology to support you and your goals. With more qualified applicants in the talent pool today, recruiters report that innovations in recruitment technology are making their job easier.[XIII]

To you, this means the provider is marketing itself to job seekers through online, print and broadcast advertising, public relations, word-of-mouth campaigns, search engines and more. You are not only paying to post your ads. You are paying for your online partner to bring the right job seekers to apply to your jobs.

Benefits of online hourly recruitment

Maximum exposure: Job websites have growing and diverse audiences, with more than 166 million unique users visiting the top job boards each month—that's more than five million each day.

Cost-cutting advantages: Online recruitment sites offer greater posting visibility with fewer overhead costs, delivering greater value than traditional advertising methods. Many job boards offer discounts when you buy in bulk, enhancing your economics.

Higher caliber candidates: Employment websites generally offer tools that can help filter out unqualified job seekers, ultimately generating quality, pre-screened candidates. Better qualified candidates improve your interview-to-hire ratio, and lower your cost-per-hire and turnover rate. Plus, unlike traditional recruitment methods, you always know how many qualified applicants result directly from your online postings. In addition, job seekers are screening themselves as they go online and navigate the application process.

Learn more about applicant screening in Chapter 6, Screening for Right-Fit Hires.

Job descriptions that make sense: With newspaper classified ads, you pay by the word or line, which adds up quickly and often limits what you can say about your company and job. Online advertising gives you greater flexibility to craft accurate and robust job descriptions, often at a fraction of the cost.

Targeted service: Newspaper classified ad representatives may deal with everything from the "help wanted" to "used car" entries. With an employment website, you'll find staff with unique expertise in developing on-brand job descriptions that effectively look and sound like your business and what you do.

– SnagAJob.com

You'll never play hide and seek online with hourly seekers.

One of the questions that we encounter most frequently is whether people looking for hourly jobs are online. They are. We've previously mentioned that low-income households—the primary target audience for hourly employment—represent the fastest-growing online segment. This doesn't simply comprise students and those looking to supplement the family income with part-time jobs. According to SnagAJob.com polling, 56 percent of all people coming to SnagAJob.com are looking for full-time hourly jobs.

And hourly job seekers aren't just online; they're reaching the web through high-speed Internet access. We've found that 93 percent of SnagAJob.com traffic comes from broadband users. In fact, for many hourly jobs, one of the preliminary screenings you will have is whether applicants are comfortable with operating a computer, a digital cash register or diagnostic equipment—whether in a medical setting or auto repair center. Finding potential hires through online recruiting can help you pre-screen job seekers as they demonstrate whether they have the basic technology skills you need on the job.

Make sure **the brand stands tall.**

As you build recruitment partnerships, you need to maintain control over your brand—who and what your company represents. You can partner with an online recruitment source in different ways. You may opt to make job seekers aware of your positions on a job board—but direct them to your company website to apply. You might send a job feed to vertical search engines, which could be two or more steps away from your company website. No matter where—and why—you send job seekers en route to becoming applicants, here are a few things to keep in mind:

Make it easy: Remember that the more hoops you ask job seekers to jump through, the greater the chance that they'll abandon the application process.

Display road signs: If you're taking job seekers to multiple sites, and the transitions aren't visually seamless, make sure you let people know that they're on your site, a partnering job board, etc. If job seekers get lost, they're likely to hop lanes to another website.

Shorten the commute: If you wait more than 48 hours before responding to job seekers, your best applicants may be unavailable. Be sure to also respond to those you don't extend an employment offer to, as there is a good chance they're also your customers.

Mind the gaps: Look for drop-off rates in the application flow and patch up the processes.

Play traffic cop: As hourly job seekers complete your online application, add a question that asks how candidates heard about your job. This will help determine your best hourly recruitment mix.

Something else to remember when co-branding: in your recruitment partnerships, make sure the way you talk about your business and the use of graphics is true to your company, no matter how much a recruitment partner's style might contrast with your own. And be sure to paint an engaging 3D image of your culture in a consistent manner across all recruitment channels. The content and composition of your job descriptions can be an unparalleled accelerant for boosting your qualified applicant traffic, as you'll learn over the next several pages.

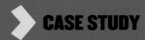

Boston Market: Rethinking Hourly Recruiting

OPPORTUNITY: Boston Market was using the traditional recruitment channels to find new store employees: newspaper ads, referrals and "Now Hiring" signs posted in the window. But company leaders recognized an emerging opportunity for identifying candidates who matched their hiring demographics. "We knew online was where they were going to be looking for jobs," says Jason Lessman, manager of recruiting and HR systems.

> What matters most is "not the amount of [applicant] flow. It's the quality of the flow... We strive to avoid filling up our general managers' emails with unqualified candidates."

SOLUTION: Reshaping its recruitment strategy to incorporate online recruiting would enable Boston Market to streamline hiring practices for its store managers, reinforce the corporate message of being a great restaurant to work for, and connect with job seekers who may not walk into a location to apply.

In 2001, Boston Market began posting its open jobs on SnagAJob.com, implementing a best practice that makes it easy for interested job seekers to find them and apply. They developed attractive job postings that promote the benefits of working for Boston Market, including growth opportunities, and created a handful of screening questions that allow applicants to quickly share their core skill sets. Completed job seeker profiles and applications are automatically sent via email to hiring managers at the locations to which seekers applied. "For the tool to work, you need to check on it every day," Lessman says. "Hourly workers have a lot of options to choose from; if you don't catch them quickly, they're going to go down the street to someone else."

RESULTS: Online recruiting is generating up to 30,000 hourly candidates per month. Strategic screening questions such as minimum age requirements help the restaurant company focus only on qualified candidates, which represent about 30 percent of initial applicants. Last year, Boston Market hired 5,800 new employees through SnagAJob.com. What matters most is "not the amount of [applicant] flow," he says. "It's the quality of the flow...We strive to avoid filling up our general managers' emails with unqualified candidates."

An additional benefit is that Boston Market is building a consistent brand image nationally, rather than risking disconnected marketing efforts by its local general managers. Candidates now receive the same core message about what makes Boston Market both a great workplace and a great restaurant. "Candidates want to work for a company that has a solid reputation," Lessman says.

Creating Best-Selling Job Descriptions

> **Engage job seekers from the get-go with page-turning perks** and by creating a peephole into your company culture.

While crafting top-notch job descriptions can take a extra little time up front, the pay-off is superior applications, more efficient screening and better prepared applicants. The additional upshot is that managers can use their time in a smarter manner, and your recruitment is ultimately more cost-efficient.

What sets job descriptions apart in the online world is:

Prime real estate: More room to describe your business and what you do, including more details about jobs across multiple locations.

Full disclosure: More clarity about the duties and responsibilities of your jobs and what you are looking for in top candidates.

Deeper inside look: More details (and even anecdotes) on the benefits of what makes your company a great place to work.

Bells and whistles: Images, design elements, videos and interactive tools to create more engaging job postings.

Posting jobs online delivers immediate tangible gains, such as a more cost-effective use of recruitment budgets. Other benefits include: more right-fit candidates, company brand building and increased customer base.

Online recruitment also delivers significant intangible rewards. For example, by promoting your diversity of jobs, you illustrate potential career advancement opportunities within your company.

Basic elements of effective online job descriptions

Company description: Provide a snapshot of your company and what it does. Remember that you are competing with every other employer for job seekers, so try to make your business stand out.

Corporate culture: Give an insider's view of what it's like to work for your company and daily life there. If possible, let current employees add their voices (and faces) to this piece.

Job title: Scrub your internal job names and describe the job by its function; you need to use language common to everyone to increase the probability that job seekers find your job. If you're hiring for multiple jobs at one location, link them all in each posting: Your candidate may find a job that's a better match, which may even be a tougher one for you to fill.

Job duties: Detail the key tasks for each job; make sure that applicants know exactly what is required in the role.

Pay and benefits: Offer solid information about pay and benefits. The more specific you are—for example, including actual pay rates—the more applications you generate. You also want to promote benefits such as medical coverage, tuition reimbursement, flexible schedules and other workplace perks if they're competitive within your industry.

Location: Give the exact location of the job. More than 80 percent of hourly job seekers won't travel farther than 10 miles—or as far as public transportation takes them—to get to work, according to SnagAJob.com research.

Basic requirements: List "must-have" qualifications for the job, such as legal age requirements or professional certifications.

Advancement: Show hourly applicants the appropriate job ladder, and what advanced job opportunities lie a rung away.

Make your job postings an open book about who you are.
And don't forget pretty pictures.

You are looking for qualified people who are searching for jobs right now. Your online postings should start with the basics. Give job seekers a robust and accurate description of your business and your jobs.

Don't stop there. Remember, part of the reason to invest in online postings is more space (at significantly lower costs) to tell people what you do and why you do it. Use it purposefully. Every word should add value and reinforce your brand, rather than simply work to fill up white space.

Writing powerful job descriptions for online readers may require some mental adjustments. You and your recruitment teams have honed your ability to pack full descriptions into the fewest words possible to make traditional advertising affordable for you. On your corporate website, you may be used to providing more task-oriented job descriptions that are a few clicks away from any messaging about your corporate culture or the benefits of working for your company. You also want to think about your approach to writing an hourly job description vs. a salaried career description. SnagAJob.com research shows that hourly job seekers of all ages prefer easy access to wage details and job descriptions formatted for quick and easy scanning.

Fresh job descriptions yield ripe candidates

In the following excerpt, see how using friendly language and including an attractive employee benefit can immediately punch up the effectiveness of your job descriptions:

Bad:	Good:
Ass't. DP for cyr. mfr. wanted for wkdy PT empl	**Package Tech is seeking an assistant data processing technician for its manufacturing operation. The part-time, weekday position includes vacation time, bonus pay, and a fun and casual work environment.**

Notice how little things like calling out the company by name lends instant credibility to the second description. Plus, when you post jobs online, you can get your message across clearly since you're not paying per word.

What do job seekers look for in online job descriptions?

QUICK READABILITY	10%
PICTURES & VIDEO	2%
WAGE DETAILS	27%
PERKS & BENEFITS	5%
JOB DETAILS	55%

– SnagAJob.com

Postings on job boards allow job seekers to find out what they want to know about your company, your workplace and your jobs on a single page. Depending on the capabilities of your online recruitment partner, you can provide additional links within a job board to a broader company profile.

To start building your recruitment brand, think about how you market yourself to your customers. In many ways, the very people who use your company for goods or services—from eating at your restaurant to those buying clothes in your store—are a starting point for finding prospective employees. People return to your business because you deliver on what you promise your customers. You should do the same with your employees.

"Every business wants to mirror its community," says Martin Riggs, a 20-year HR professional and former director of shared service recruiting for Brinker International, whose restaurants include Chili's Grill & Bar, Romano's Macaroni Grill, On the Border Mexican Grill & Cantina, and Maggiano's Little Italy.

Look at how you position your company to interact with your customers. In the restaurant business, you might present an environment that is warm and inviting to your guests. Does that tone extend to prospective applicants in your job postings, recruitment materials and overall application experience—whether it's at the hostess stand or online? "If they don't get that feeling when they walk in, you've already lost a little credibility in that candidate's eyes," Riggs says. "We represent our brand wherever we are."

Remember that a single job posting is the foundation for developing long-term relationships with prospective employees. "Employee engagement starts when they decide to apply to your company," Riggs adds.

▶ Create a reflecting pool of job descriptions that allows your culture to shine through.

What you say about your business—and what others say—is what gets customers and applicants in your door. "If you are clear about what you do and how you do it, you're going to attract the right people," says Joni Doolan Thomas, founder and CEO of People Report, the leading benchmarking firm in the foodservice sector.

JOB DESCRIPTIONS

Don't Sell Your Jobs Short

You need to communicate in ways that speak to different audiences, according to hourly recruitment insider Martin Riggs. College students, for example, may want higher wages, fewer hours and the option to work at the same company both at home and at school. "That may not be what appeals to the full-time hourly worker who is looking for benefits and development," he says. "They see that as a path for moving into a management role." Pay drives hourly workers in their job search, but other factors are also important.

This chart is just one example, but here's the point: If you offer any perks, make sure they're effectively conveyed in your job postings so you can attract job seekers with assorted wants and needs.

Other benefits to tout include employee discounts, tuition reimbursements, medical benefits, referral incentives, free training and even an outdoor work environment. Be sure to occasionally survey employees to check to see if the benefits you offer are what they're really looking for or if there are others that might be more appealing—and possibly more cost-effective for you. This feedback is relatively easy to obtain and priceless for maintaining optimal retention.

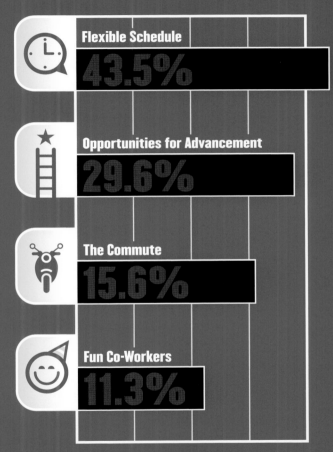

Flexible Schedule
43.5%

Opportunities for Advancement
29.6%

The Commute
15.6%

Fun Co-Workers
11.3%

– SnagAJob.com

The corporate vision and brand should drive how you write your job descriptions. For example, Chipotle has become a hip, energetic company known for using fresh, organic and, if available, local products in its menu of Tex-Mex offerings. After dusk at Denny's, the crowd is more casual and relaxed. Both companies apply that knowledge to tailor their recruiting, Thomas notes. Chipotle built its campaign to attract people with emotional connections to its sustainability cause, while Denny's traded in the third-shift uniform for jeans and turned up the rock music. Those tactics work because they reflect the people who see themselves as customers at those restaurants.

"As you slice and dice your potential employment market, you need to understand what appeals to which potential candidate pool," Thomas adds. Build some excitement and exclusivity that helps your ideal candidates see themselves—and only themselves—at your company. "You want your jobs to be unique and individual," Thomas says. "If it's too easy to get, then candidates may not want to get in there."

Nonconformity and truth will help your postings stick out and resonate with relevant job seekers.

To make real gains in your recruitment strategies, step out of conventional thinking about employment ads and embrace the versatility that online postings deliver. Recruitment strategies reinforce your brand by targeted use of your corporate typeface, logos and workplace photos. Bring all that together in a way that job seekers can immediately see themselves at your business.

Don't neglect job posting basic training.

Before you get all creative in your hourly job postings, remember that more than half of job seekers admit to not reading job descriptions in their entirety. Be sure to have an impactful (and truthful) headline, and use bullets and subheadings to make your descriptions easy on the eye. Once you've grabbed job seekers' attention, sell the job by explaining the nitty-gritty about your open position and the company.

Create a sense of community that grabs hourly workers' attention.

Online job seekers want more information about potential employers. Blind "help wanted" ads aren't effective on the Internet. For example, don't just tell job seekers that you are a restaurant in need of cooks. Take the space available with online job postings to talk about what kind of restaurant you are and how your passionate people deliver on your service promise to your customers. You can even have employees engage job seekers in various online community settings.

Draw the spotlight on yourself in a crowded marketplace.

Focus on what sets you and your jobs apart. If you pay higher-than-average hourly wages, have an extra fun work atmosphere, train your workers or offer medical benefits, then showcase that information prominently in your descriptions. If it's career growth, detail the professional paths within your company. And make it real. Don't just say you have a "fun and exciting" workplace: Tell people what makes it fun and exciting to work for your company. Better yet, have your team of employees share their stories. Do you have a winning workplace softball team? A monthly karaoke happy hour after closing? Or maybe even a strong partnership with a local nonprofit that serves as inspiration for your employees? These are all benefits you should tout.

Speak the language that is meaningful for hourly job seekers.

Recognize the fine balance between differentiating your workplace and making it hard for job seekers to find your job. Avoid industry jargon in writing your job descriptions. Bottom line: Use plain English. For example, a job seeker who wants to work at the check-out line in a local store will most likely type in the term "cashier" into Google to find open jobs. Don't hide your jobs from potential candidates by clinging to internal lingo, such as "transaction clerk."

Leave job seekers high-tech bread crumbs

That's where Search Engine Optimization (SEO) comes into play. At its most basic, SEO is about using the right words so that search engines (e.g., Google and Yahoo!) can find your jobs—whether on your company website or a partnering job board. The better the match between the words in your job postings and the terms that people are searching for right now, the higher your site and/or jobs appear when search results are returned. When you use words that resonate with both your job seekers and the major search engines, including Google and Yahoo!, you're winning the SEO battle.

To make that happen quickly and efficiently, use simple, natural language in your job descriptions—words that have meaning for job seekers looking online for jobs. You want to use key terms repeatedly to describe, in layman's terms, what your current job opening is. Hourly workers most often are searching by location and function, so you should use that information prominently in your online job description. There are several applications you can use and even SEO experts and consultants you can hire to help boost organic search performance if you don't have in-house resources. Much of this is done behind the scenes of the website infrastructure, and includes optimizing invisible metadata and tags. Odds are, your competition already has their jobs streamlined for the search engines, so be sure to check out how their job descriptions are being ranked compared to yours. And while you're looking at numbers, be sure to plug in to a number of free and paid SEO tools that can show you preferred search terms to use. For example, do more job seekers search for open positions using the term "clerk" or "cashier"? These resources will guide you to the right answer.

If you partner with a job board, the team there will help you incorporate the right key words that enhance the probability of seekers finding your jobs. Those same job boards have their own independent SEO efforts to bring users to their site, which, in turn, filters down to your jobs and job descriptions.

Words with meaning for hourly job seekers

Ineffective	Effective	What you gain by changing your words
Team Member	Cook, mechanic, housekeeper, etc.	Describes the actual job that you are looking to fill.
Restaurant Expo	Restaurant line crew, food runner, etc.	Helps to better explain your industry specific titles in basic terminology everyone can understand.
Transaction Clerk	Cashier	Trades your corporate speak or industry jargon for plain English.
Off-price Market	Discount store	Reflects how people see your business.
Anytown, USA	123 Main Street	Tells precisely where a job seeker would be working.
Opportunities Available Here	A listing of your current job openings	Captures job seekers who can apply for relevant jobs.

Open the door and show people what makes you great.

More real estate and full color on the Internet allow you to draw job seekers right into your business. Show your workplace and the types of people who work there. With more hourly workers now accessing the Internet through high-speed access—consider adding a company video to bring your workplace to life, including asking your current employees to explain, in their own words, about what makes your business a great workplace.

Learn more about using video in job description, as well as targeting postings, in Chapter 9, Taking It to the Next Level.

Write once—recruit always.

Put your job descriptions to work for you. Depending on your business, you probably face ongoing needs to hire for a core group of positions. Retailers need cashiers and stockroom employees. Hotels need housekeepers and desk clerks. In other businesses, your common and ongoing volume of hiring may be for security guards, tellers or drivers. Review your new hires over the past six months or year to identify the roles for which you have made the most hires. Use your analysis to build a library of common job descriptions. When special needs come up, adapt those templates for seasonal work, unique locations, teens or other market segments. Depending on your technical capabilities, and those of your online recruitment partners, you may even be able to tailor messaging and content for individual job seekers as they arrive at your postings to target specific attributes. For example, if one job seeker is applying for your location in Boston and another is applying for your location in Los Angeles, wouldn't you like to be able to tailor the job information and even complementary visuals to match the unique characteristics of these two workplaces—and the applicants they're each likely to attract?

 ### Fill your hourly recruitment pipeline. And turn the valve on as needed.

One of the biggest missed opportunities with online job postings is that businesses quickly forget about revamping and reloading. Build time into your recruitment schedule to refresh your active online ads. As you hire strong new people, reserve time to review their experiences and skills so that you understand what differentiates them from others in the market. Revise your job descriptions to attract and capture candidates with similar shared characteristics. At the same time, strive for a diverse pool of workers to create a truly eclectic workplace.

With many job boards, you pay for a 30-day job posting, so be ready for a steady stream of job seekers during that lifecycle. In fact, many larger businesses keep their postings active year-round to ensure an ongoing candidate flow for positions that are often open. Unlike a print advertisement that is out of sight once the newspaper lands in the recycling bin, your online job posting has a longer shelf life and greater opportunity to be seen by more job seekers. If you're a small business needing only a single hire, you can immediately deactivate your posting to ensure you're not wasting time dealing with and turning away interested parties.

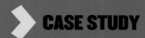
Kohl's: Creating Best-Selling Job Descriptions

OPPORTUNITY: Kohl's—the national value-oriented specialty department store, based in Menomonee Falls, WI.— knows that its customers are its best future workers. That's why it looks for in-store marketing strategies to invite customers to come work for the retailer as hourly workers, with a focus on cashiers, floor representatives and stockers. Those include running ads over the public-address system and posting "now hiring" signs at the front doors.

SOLUTION: While shoppers may not be ready to halt their errands and apply right then and there, online applications enable candidates to seek out a Kohl's job when it is most convenient for them. Kohl's online postings also reinforce the benefits of working there, including computer and peer training and generous discounts on store merchandise. An initial online candidate screening "tells us a little more about whether that individual would be a good fit," says Vanessa Vigil, an assistant store manager.

> Directly appealing to its customers matches the store's needs with its commitment to providing quality customer service.

When a new store is scheduled to open, Kohl's augments that strategy with career fairs that attract volumes of applicants to fill out its hiring.

"You have the opportunity to pick out the cream of the crop," says Glenda Leonard, an assistant store manager.

RESULTS: Directly appealing to its customers matches the store's needs with its commitment to providing quality customer service. As customers, these individuals are familiar with the store's products and selections—and how the store respects and treats its shoppers. However, even in a tough market for hourly workers, the company knows that its top talent provides the level of customer service that differentiates Kohl's from other retailers. "If the candidate is not customer-oriented—no matter how hard of a worker that individual may promise to be—we need to pass," Leonard says.

From the corner store to the corner office: creating bestselling job descriptions

Go online and change how you talk about your company and your jobs. Make sure you understand your company's brand, then write fresh job descriptions that reflect it. Keep in mind that the more you can disclose up front about pay, benefits and culture, the more effective your posting will be in finding right-fit candidates. And don't be afraid to tout the inherent perks of small businesses, including the close-knit family atmosphere.

Build a pool of effective online descriptions for the jobs for which you hire most. As you know, your hiring needs will be ongoing, and you want to create a steady pipeline of qualified job seekers. You should also ensure that your corporate profile is current and provides a visual snapshot of your business.

Take a look at the traits and skills of your best employees. Review your current online job descriptions to ensure they include those model traits and experiences as you look for new people to join your team. Explore ways to expand your corporate brand, such as adding workplace videos and creating customized content.

Job descriptions as a second language

Do you think like your job seekers? Better yet, do you write and talk like your job seekers? Many words and phrases you use regularly may not be in the wheelhouse of your target job seeker demographic, but instead comprise jargon and corporate language. Add clarity and translate the underlined words in each of the following examples into friendlier language that will more effectively connect with your job applicants.

Candidates need at least three years experience managing <u>shrink control</u>

Now hiring for <u>Expo positions</u>

Applicants needed with <u>split schedule</u> availability

Local <u>warehouse club</u> seeks third-shift manager

Take advantage of our <u>Employee Purchase Plan</u> after 30 days

Using online recruitment tools

Fill out the chart on the following pages to reveal your company's strengths and weaknesses.

Your company	Describe your current tactics
Corporate Website	
General Job Board	
Niche Job Board	
Social Networking Site	
Vertical Search Engines/ Job Aggregators	

Now enter the same info for your competitors, which can be found everywhere from their corporate website to Google news searches and industry blogs. Once you've completed those two sections, pore over, break down and search for opportunities—tactics your competition is using that you've yet to take up.

Your competitor	Describe your competitors' tactics
Corporate Website	
General Job Board	
Niche Job Board	
Social Networking Site	
Vertical Search Engines/ Job Aggregators	

Put everything together and recruit top talent.

After you complete the following exercises, use your competitive research, along with what you learned from the exercise, to write a new job description based on the job seekers' perspectives. Be sure to use this opportunity to talk about your company and what you do, the benefits of working for you and specific duties of the job. By following this model, you'll be ready to submit your posting and anticipate a steady flow of qualified applications in less time than you think.

Write effective job descriptions for your business.

What are your three most common open positions?

Review your hiring records over the past year to identify the roles that you have filled—or sought to fill—most often.

1.

2.

3.

Study your competition.

Now choose one of your most common open positions and pull out the job description you're currently using. Go online to a competitor's website or a general or niche job board to find a posting for a similar job. Fill in the chart below with information for both you and your competitor, paying close attention to how each of you leverages your perks and benefits.

Your competitor	**Position:** _____
Company description	
Job title	
Functional duties	
Location	
Pay	
Benefits	
"Must haves" minimum age, certification requirements	
Corporate logo or imagery	
Extras (employee testimonials, etc.)	

Update the elements of your job description.

Now that you've done some homework about how your competitors are looking for the same top job seekers, rethink how you tell potential employees about your open job. Start by using your current company information listed in the first exercise. Now, take a step back and think about your brand and how to better tell people outside your company about what makes this a great job and a great place to work. Don't forget to consider how the best candidates will search for your job online, so put aside the recruiting or corporate-speak and use words that have meaning to your candidates.

Your current job description	Position: _____
Company description	
Job title	
Functional duties	
Location	
Pay	
Benefits	
"Must haves" minimum age, certification requirements	
Corporate logo or imagery	
Extras (employee testimonials, etc.)	

Your improved job description   Position: _____

Company description	
Job title	
Functional duties	
Location	
Pay	
Benefits	
"Must haves" minimum age, certification requirements	
Corporate logo or imagery	
Extras (employee testimonials, etc.)	

Sources

I   CareerXRoads. "CareerXRoads 7th Annual Source of Hire Study: What 2007 Results Mean for Your 2008 Plans," Gerry Crispin and Mark Mehler. Kendall Park, N.J., 2008.

II   U.S. Department of Commerce, Economics and Statistics Administration, National Telecommunications and Information Administration. "A Nation Online: Entering the Broadband Age." Washington, D.C., September 2004.

III WEDDLE's. "Weddle's Annual Source of Employment Survey." 27 March 2008, http://www.weddles.com/recruiternews/issue.cfm?Newsletter=226>

IV   Davidson, Barbara. "Hiring an Employee: How Much Does It Cost?" Workforce Management: http://www.workforce.com/archive/feature/22/25/58/223946.php.

V   DeutscheBank Research, June 2004

VI   Borrell Associates. "2007 Outlook: Online Recruitment Advertising." Williamsburg, Va., 2007.

VII Borrell Associates. "2008 Outlook: Online Recruitment Advertising." Williamsburg, Va., 2008.

VIII WEDDLE's. "The Six Habits of Ineffective Recruiters." 3 April 2008. <http://www.weddles.com/recruiternews/issue.cfm?Newsletter=227>.

IX   Pew Internet & American Life Project. "Demographics of Internet Users." 2007 October 24-December 2. <http://www.pewinternet.org/trends/User_Demo_2.15.08.htm.>

X   SnagAJob.com

XI   Spherion. "Workplace Snapshot Survey: MySpace Resume Post." 10 October 2006. <http:www.spherion.com/press/releases/2006/snapshot_my_space.jsp>

XII Berta, Dina. "Restaurant Players Address Younger Employees' Online Habits via Interactive Crew-Only Websites." Nation's Restaurant News. 19 May 2008: 1.

XIII DirectEmployers Association. "2006 DirectEmployers Association Recruiting Trends Survey," Booz Allen Hamilton. Washington, D.C., 2006.

Notes

CHAPTER 6

Screening for Right-Fit Hires

Once you lock in on your ideal hourly candidates, don't just close your eyes and pull the trigger. You're only halfway there.

You have two strong and strategic opportunities to maximize technology in screening large volumes of candidates:

Ask your "knock-out" questions as soon as the bell rings.

Within your initial online application, include a few key screening questions that are critical to matching candidates with must-have requirements for your jobs. Consider these questions a pre-interview stage. If the candidates don't match those basic and unwavering requirements, you don't have to invest valuable time in reviewing the qualifications of people you won't be hiring for those roles.

Put your candidates to the test with technology and online assessments.

You know the skills and behaviors that people need to succeed in your jobs. In-depth online assessments allow you to predict the performance of candidates against the responsibilities they would find in your business. While these forms can take a little time to complete, serious candidates readily accept this opportunity to prove their ability to meet your job requirements.

Online screening questions and assessments drive efficiency in your overall recruitment strategy. After all, time is money for your organization. With many hourly managers trying to balance ongoing hiring needs with the day-to-day demands of the business—and the immediate customer crisis always wins out—they need tools that help them focus quickly on job seekers who rise to the top of the talent pool. Let's take this one step further and mention something we can't say enough: Managing these efficiencies doesn't just boost the retention rate of your frontline workforce; it also keeps your managers on board longer.

Managing hourly worker expectations.

Hourly job applicants have a need for speed. According to SnagAJob.com research, 56 percent of hourly job seekers expect to hear back from employers within 48 hours of submitting their applications. In addition, our own findings have shown that 37 percent of hourly job seekers say getting hired quickly is the most important factor when looking for a job. What's it all mean? It means that your hiring managers also have a need for speed.

 **QUICK READ**

Incorporate strategic questions into the application to immediately screen out people who don't meet your "must-have" conditions.

Use online assessments to quickly and efficiently find candidates who match the targeted behaviors and skills for your jobs.

Track the quality of your new hires and use that knowledge to refine your hiring process.

Good to Know!

How not to lose out on the best hourly candidates

- **Trigger an automated response as soon as online applications are submitted that accomplishes the following:**
  - Confirms application receipt.
  - Sets specific expectations for response timeframe and method.

- **Plan how and when you'll review applications:**
  - Set aside time every day.
  - Employ a quick turnaround. Top SnagAJob.com clients report best results from responding within 24–48 hours.

- **Be consistent with second-screening tactics, whether it's a phone call, interview, etc.**

- **Be sure to contact applicants you're not pursuing, too. They're potentially loyal customers or know someone who is, so be respectful.**

- **Prepare frontline workers to handle applicants following up in person at your location.**

Hourly workers may not have resumés, but they often have experiences—just give them a chance to tell you about them.

One of the biggest differences between hourly and salaried workers is that hourly workers often don't have resumés. With many generally looking for entry-level or part-time roles, they simply haven't had the need to compile a full resumé.

Effective online applications create opportunities for job seekers to detail their experience in ways that are meaningful to them and your recruiting team. To start, keep an open mind on what experience means as you start to review your hourly candidates. You can't approach the hourly job seeker population as a homogenous group. Instead, you find high school students who may have leadership experience with a school club or government association; former stay-at-home moms looking to return to the workforce with experience now coming from PTA or volunteer roles; and 55-plus workers looking for part-time jobs to keep busy during retirement—but perhaps not in their career field of, say, engineering or business, where they have decades of experience.

Your online application on a job board should give step-by-step directions that guide job seekers in building profiles that capture their different career and life experiences, particularly as they are relevant to your work. Even if you use your corporate site and a Talent Management System (TMS), you should tailor your online application to reflect how hourly workers traditionally describe their experiences, rather than asking detailed questions about advanced education and requiring them to submit a formal resumé. Your strategy for reviewing hourly candidate profiles should start with building a framework that captures what this talent pool has to offer:

Allow job seekers to tell you their story and what sets them apart. Give them a chance to tell you about their experience. They may tell you more about what they can do—the practical talents they can bring to your company—than where they have worked, and that's essential information that you can use in matching applicants to your open jobs.

Open and Close the
Screening Door

Ask questions that allow applicants to tell you about themselves:

Bad:
Have you ever worked in a restaurant?

Good:
What experience do you have in providing exceptional customer service?

Bad:
Do you have a good driving record?

Good:
Do you have have a valid Class A CDL and have you ever been convicted of any driving infractions?

Remember what differentiates your hourly candidates. These job seekers are looking for jobs and paychecks right now. If your application is too cumbersome or extensive, you might lose some candidates who quickly move on to other opportunities. Focus on making it easy. For example, rather than having applicants fill in the same information in multiple screens, pre-populate that data into fields after they've filled it out the first time. (Remember that the actual online application process itself also serves as a critical screen, as you find the job seekers who complete the process are truly interested and want to work for you.) And if they're completing an online application, they're likely demonstrating they have some technical savvy.

Ask the right questions up front and save yourself time (and frustration).

Succeeding in the hourly marketplace requires strategic thinking. Just as in your business, you need to study and understand your market: hourly job seekers. These candidates don't approach their job search in the same way as salaried workers, so you shouldn't approach how you recruit them the same way either.

As an example, consider the differences between your average hourly and salaried application. The approach hourly job seekers take and the content they produce comprises more than subtle nuances when compared to their salaried counterparts. Be sure you're taking the opportunity to sniff out the clues for truly understanding and appreciating what hourly candidates bring to the table.

Going online with the application process, including introducing those initial "knock-out" screening questions, can be the first step in developing an automated recruitment strategy that delivers efficiency and effectiveness. In addition to throwing these knock-out punches inquiring about "must-have" skills or experience, you also want to pepper applicants with "nice-to-have" informational questions. Both of these lines of questioning are essential, whether or not you have an hourly recruitment process automated through technology.

Panning for
Golden
Candidates?

Ask general knock-out questions:
Bartender:
Are you at least X years of age?

Warehouse worker:
Can you lift at least X pounds at a time?

Ask informational/"nice-to-have" questions:
Bartender:
Are you available to work holidays?

Warehouse worker:
Do you have X years experience driving a forklift?

Reading an hourly job seeker profile or application

What you see	What that might mean
Internship/volunteer experience	Job seeker may be looking for a first job. Could end up having great work ethic or leadership skills.
Gap in employment history	Applicant may be listing only experience directly related to your job listing, such as waitressing gigs for a restaurant job; they may have other pertinent customer service experience from retail. This may also be a parent returning to the workforce or taking care of family.
Notes that friend or family recommended your company	Job seeker has been told about why it's great to work at your company and has specifically sought you out.

– SnagAJob.com

▶ Consistency mixed with technology yields a potent recruitment cocktail.

Now that you've screened out clear "non-fit candidates," ask a few more targeted questions.

"Automating the process is important and can deliver some savings, but the big benefits will come when you start looking at who you are hiring," says Steve Earl, director of marketing for the Talent Management Division of Kronos Incorporated. The Chelmsford, MA-based firm empowers organizations around the world with technology solutions to effectively manage their workforce.

With little debate, most companies with significant hourly worker populations stress that the volatility of this market segment and high turnover rates reinforce the critical nature of making right-fit hires from the start. Kronos comes at that challenge with a

The Talent
Management System
Advantage:

- 82 percent of hiring managers credit technology as the most important step they have taken to address the sourcing, ranking and hiring processes.
- More than 50 percent of hiring managers say that integrating the various pieces of their current hiring systems had a positive impact on their businesses.

– Aberdeen Group study, March 2005[II]

scientific team that looks at shared characteristics among top-performing employees, particularly in hourly roles that it describes as "field workers."

A TMS has assessment tools that can be tailored according to job responsibilities. But a company needs to start with a clear understanding of the knowledge, skills and abilities demonstrated by their top employees in those positions today. The Kronos model helps companies develop custom assessments that enable you to:

- Identify qualified candidates quickly and reliably.
- Select the right people for the right jobs systematically.
- Optimize manager accountability in the selection process.[I]

Within a 45-minute session, companies can ask a slate of strategic questions that capture valuable information, with a focus on assessing a candidate's safety, service and skills. "What we're trying to do is identify people who fit best," Earl says. "You can't get that from a couple of questions. You need to ask the right questions to get useful data. Science is how we build the tools to help hiring managers predict the abilities of their candidates."

Assessments provide an objective and comparable set of information that hiring managers can use in deciding which candidates to interview. Companies with more comprehensive talent management systems can provide an online snapshot of every applicant's testing performance and other related hiring information.

Your hiring needs don't end when your newest employee arrives for the first day of work. You need to keep a pipeline flowing of qualified candidates.

Without question, one of the greatest challenges in managing an hourly workforce is the high volume of turnover, where a business that reports a 100 percent turnover rate means it is replacing its entire workforce in a single year. For many businesses, that means a constant part of the job is finding the next waitress for a franchise burger joint, a phone agent for the company service center or a cashier to check out department store customers.

FOODSERVICE EMPLOYEE TURNOVER:

Hourly, by Restauraunt Type (2007)

151%

123%

102%

89%

Quick
Service

Fast Casual
Family Dining

Casual
Dining

High Volume
Fine Dining

– People Report III

Management & Hourly 1997–2007

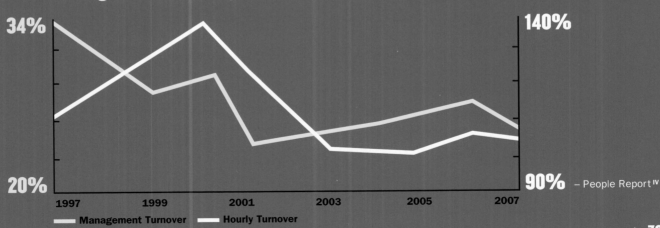

34%

140%

20%

90% – People Report IV

1997   1999   2001   2003   2005   2007

— Management Turnover   — Hourly Turnover

According to People Report, the average employee turnover rate in hourly industries is 106 percent compared to 27 percent in salaried industries, an indication that most hourly employees will likely stay on the job for less than a year. And turnover means money. People Report, which specializes in foodservice industry benchmarking, notes that it costs more than $2,000 to replace an hourly employee and more than $19,000 to replace a manager. For a 100-unit company, every point you save in hourly turnover means $205,000 in cost savings.[v]

By adding filtering tools and automation, you not only find qualified applicants faster, but you can better target candidates who are more likely to stick around for a while.

> ### No matter how you find potential candidates, you need to ensure that every component of your recruitment strategy complies with government regulations.

In coming to work each day, you are rightly focused on the product or service that your company delivers to the marketplace. However, you also need to provide appropriate attention to how you manage that business, beginning with your employees—whether you are hiring your first worker or your workforce totals tens of thousands.

Over the years, employment laws and regulations have evolved to ensure fair treatment of workers. By complying with the appropriate regulations, you ensure that you are offering a fair workplace for your employees—and minimizing your risk of employee lawsuits or government penalties. This is just another reason to embrace new technology in your hourly recruitment; automation drives standardization and ensures consistent compliancy.

Remember that while new human resources technology and software can streamline and automate much of your work, you need to ensure that your systems still maintain your obligations. If you ever have a question about your employment practices and regulatory requirements, you should consult with your legal adviser.

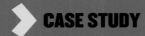

Potbelly Sandwich Works: Screening for Right-Fit Hires

OPPORTUNITY: In the late 1990s, Potbelly Sandwich Works was a small Chicago-based company with three stores and a ton of growth potential. At that early stage, corporate leaders saw the opportunity to differentiate Potbelly's hourly workforce. The company decided to focus on finding employees who are passionate about delivering the quality service and experience that defines the Potbelly brand, and empowering workers to make sure all customers leave happy. "We needed to put a large focus and some structure around our hourly recruiting," says Carrie Luxem, director of human resources at Potbelly Sandwich Works. "Our associates have the biggest impact on our customer experience so we knew we needed to think outside the box when recruiting, selecting and hiring our hourly associates."

> "When you set the right parameters, you can focus on hiring people who really care about your customers and your company."

SOLUTION: With over 200 locations and hiring volumes growing, Potbelly turned to online recruitment to generate a pipeline of candidates that's funneled directly to local hiring managers. A cornerstone of leveraging online job postings is ensuring that the company culture and workplace—which focuses on people, both as hourly employees and customers—is clearly defined and differentiated, helping to filter out candidates who don't share that vision. The job postings incorporate restaurant images and logos to reinforce the notion that employees enjoy the same fun environment as the customers. While the postings describe the workplace and set job expectations, Potbelly uses a company video to further illustrate a day in a life of a worker.

Potbelly uses online screening questions and two interviews to hone in on people who are trustworthy and embody integrity. Those questions may include asking candidates to explain why they want to work for Potbelly or to describe a situation in which they delivered excellent customer service. "When you focus on having the right people, everything else becomes easy," Luxem says. "We put a lot of time and energy into hiring higher quality people."

RESULTS: By continuing to fine-tune what it is looking for in candidates and adapting its screening questions, Potbelly is succeeding in finding "nice people to work in an awesome company delivering a great product," Luxem says. Strategic use of online screening tools is streamlining the volume of applications, but the quality of candidates presented to hiring managers is higher—making online postings even more cost-effective. "When you set the right parameters, you can focus on hiring people who really care about your customers and your company," she says.

From the corner store to the corner office: targeting top talent

You are busy running your business, and online recruitment can help you filter out candidates who don't meet your minimum requirements. Your time is valuable, and screening questions can help you hone right in on your ideal candidate and advance quickly into the interview stage. If you are faced with having to weed personally through a pile of applications, you may be tempted to shift attention away from making the hiring decision you need. Let your online recruitment tool do that heavy lifting for you.

As your business grows, make sure you are meeting regulatory requirements with your recruiting and hiring practices. You should consult with your legal counsel as you expand your workforce to ensure your resources, tools and practices are in compliance. You may be exercising all the necessary precautions, but are all your frontline hiring managers operating from the same book? One way to help keep up on the latest employment regulations is to join your national or local trade association, which can provide updates that apply specifically to your industry and help you mitigate potential legal risks.

Remember that the differences between hourly and salaried workers comprise much more than subtle nuances. And when you're dealing with significant populations of both hourly and salaried workers, you need to resist the temptation to use the same talent management system for both. By using a product customized for each of these groups of workers, you'll ensure that you're capturing the job seeker profile you're after.

Craft superior screening questions.

By giving job seekers a way to apply online for your open jobs, you gain an upfront and efficient opportunity to learn whether they are qualified. While you don't want to lose their interest with a barrage of questions, you can ask a few strategic questions to determine their potential match before inviting them for an interview.

Just as you are building a pool of standard job descriptions that you can post when those jobs become available, you should also create a list of standard screening questions for those positions.

What is your most common job opening?

What are the three "must-have" attributes? If you're looking for a pizza delivery driver, these might include a question about having consistent transportation.

☑ **Must have...**

☑ **Must have...**

☑ **Must have...**

Now what are three "nice-to-have" questions to further probe applicants for desired experience and skills? You might ask those same pizza delivery driver applicants whether or not they have previous relevant experience.

☑ **Nice to have...**

☑ **Nice to have...**

☑ **Nice to have...**

Are there any regulatory requirements for the position, i.e., minimum age or professional certification? If so, please list.

Use your responses to craft targeted screening questions that filter out candidates who don't meet both your minimum requirements and "nice-to-have" traits.

Your most common job opening:

Must-have condition	Possible questions	Your screening questions
Targeted shift or shift functions	Can you work weekdays from 4 p.m. to midnight? Do you have experience opening a store?	
Minimum age	Are you at least age 18? Are you at least age 21?	
Professional certification	Do you hold a current LPN license? Do you have a valid commercial driver's license (CDL)?	
Location	Are you willing and able to get to [specific location] to work?	

Nice-to-have trait	Possible questions	Your screening questions
Previous experience	Do you have at least two years experience operating a cash register? Have you previously worked as a manager?	
Business familiarity	Do you regularly shop at our store? What's one thing you would improve about our drive-thru window?	

Sources

I   Kronos Inc. "Find, Hire and Retain Top Talent: Using Technology to Fight the War for Talent." Chelmsford, Mass. 2007.

II   Aberdeen Group. "Enterprise Talent Management Benchmark Report." March 2005. 3.

III People Report. "New Economy Workforce Reality in a Bricks & Mortar World. Dallas, Texas." 2008. 23.

IV People Report. "The Trends that Drive Our Industry. Conference presentation: 2008." Teresa Siriani.

V   People Report. "New Economy Workforce Reality in a Bricks & Mortar World." Dallas, Texas. 2008. 31.

Notes

In the time it takes to read this chapter, an hourly job seeker will fill out an application and expect an answer. Are you ready to meet that expectation?

QUICK READ

Schedule interviews quickly and provide quality time for top candidates.

Sell the total job, including fun perks and benefits.

Remember, hourly workers are looking for jobs right now, and the longer you take to set up interviews, the more likely you are to lose out on the best talent in the marketplace. Many candidates who make it through your screening process have the same skills sought by your competitors, where they probably also applied. The most important lesson to take away is that you need to be proactive and go after qualified hourly candidates immediately.

In this chapter, we'll show you how to make every interview meaningful—and that's by making the interview useful to both the interviewer and interviewee. Too often, the same questions are asked with no thought given to how this experience can be customized. That needs to change.

The interview process presents two key opportunities for you, and we've organized the chapter accordingly into these two phases:

Determine whether the hourly applicant in front of you is the right fit for your job and company. Candidates can present a great package in their application, but nothing takes the place of the in-person—or even an over-the-phone—discussion. You need that live contact rather than second-hand interaction to make effective hiring decisions.

Sell your job and company to the best candidates. Don't forget that the top hourly job seekers may be pursuing multiple positions at different businesses. And they don't have time to burn. Invest the time in telling your strongest candidates about the benefits and opportunities of working for you.

Before you get started, create a consistent core of questions before the interview begins.

Once you have some interviews scheduled, take a few minutes to think through what you want to learn from those candidates. Your goal at this stage is to find out more about someone that you probably are putting at the frontline with your customers. You want to make sure you're asking questions—and recieving answers—that get to the heart of how that candidate will deliver on the job. Training staff members who want to work for you can be easy; getting insight on how potential hires will perform in situations they will face on the job is often more challenging. But this is what you are looking to learn during the interview.

Interview logistics checklist

When?
- Set up specific times in advance.
- Speed matters. Be able to accommodate applicants every day. Some of the best employers are able to interview, screen and give hourly candidates employment answers in real time.

Where?
- Be able to interview on the spot.
- Have a quiet, convenient location prepped and ready.

Avoid asking wishy-washy, "first-date" questions that have predictable answers.
Use "How do you do?" questions to establish rapport, but don't use these as more than a brief ice-breaker.

Use consistent questions for an objective interview process.
This will help you compare and contrast hourly candidates.

Allow frontline workers to participate for added perspective.
- Choose trustworthy hourly workers.
- Approve questions in advance.
- Ensure employees know their role. Clearly define what's expected, what's encouraged and what's not appropriate.

When you engage your full local team in the hiring process, you are building engagement across the team by demonstrating that you value your current employees' voices in finding future colleagues. Again, we know that strategic interviewing only takes a few extra minutes and some upfront coordination. You want each hourly worker you ultimately hire to be a fit for your culture and organization, and the interview allows you to get important information to use in deciding if the person in front of you right now is the right one.

Save valuable time and money down the road by creating meaningful encounters with hourly job seekers now.

Without question, finding people to fill your open roles takes time—and the interview stage can take a significant chunk of your day, particularly since many field workers are hired by local managers. It doesn't require much additional investment of your time to approach every interview with a strategic goal, especially when you consider that the result is a potentially better-fit hourly worker. Industry leaders repeatedly tell us that initial time investment translates into significant gains, such as a faster learning curve for on-the-job productivity and longer retention. What you do to prepare and conduct that interview is pivotal to your long-term success; don't let ongoing work demands force you to shortchange this one-time opportunity with a potential talented employee.

"When you talk to companies who do well or managers who are very successful in retaining a talented workforce, what you find is that some of it is as simple as taking time with employees," says Joni Thomas Doolin, founder and CEO of People Report. The Dallas-based company is the leading provider of workforce metrics, benchmarks, trends and best people practices for the foodservice industry.

You need to create an opportunity for hourly job seekers to tell you why they are the right candidate for you, especially for people who may just be entering the workforce. For example, a high school student may come to you without past job credentials, but you can ask about their academic or volunteer experiences. To note, school leadership can give you insight into how they will work with others to accomplish a task.

We mention this time and again: Turnover is notoriously high in the hourly worker segments. HR industry veteran Martin Riggs has seen first-hand how stores are constantly churning to fill open positions—often the same jobs. A critical but difficult step for many businesses is to step away from the temptation to fill an open role with the next person who walks in the door.

If you are making strategic investments in your sourcing efforts, such as job boards and pre-screening tools, you need to maintain your strategic approach through the interview phase. "At some point, you need to make that decision" to hold off hiring until you find the right employee, not simply an available worker, adds Riggs, whose career includes managing recruiting functions in the hourly-worker-intensive hotel, restaurant and retail industries.

> **"Some of it is as simple as taking time with employees."**
>
> – Joni Thomas Doolin, founder and CEO of *People Report*

Predict performance with a Q&A crystal ball.

Developed in the 1970s, behavioral interviewing is a technique that can help you predict how candidates will actually perform on the job. It's easy to ask candidates questions such as why they want to work for you or what experience they have. What's hard is gauging how their answers to those broad questions will translate into their success with the specific tasks and responsibilities that you would give them. For example, instead of asking, "What kind of manager would you be?" ask "When you had two or more frontline employees vie for the same management position, what and how did you tell the employee(s) who didn't get the job?" Behavioral interviewing is a three-step process that allows candidates to tell you about their past performance:

Situation: Think about the types of responsibilities or tasks that your hourly candidates will face, then ask them to describe when they faced a similar situation. You can ask them to tell you about a previous work experience, a school project or volunteer duty—as long as you can understand how their actions could apply to the workplace.

Action: Tell candidates to explain what they did in that situation. Encourage them to walk you through their actions step by step.

Result: Ask candidates what made their actions successful or what they learned in the process.

 Hit a bigger sweet spot.

Industry research shows that behavioral interviewing can be as much as five times more accurate in predicting on-the-job behavior than traditional interviewing.

Today, more than ever, hourly workers are pursuing jobs across market segments, and the skills they bring are transferrable to other industries. If you try to make a direct comparison of skills in your particular industry, you may be overlooking the best qualified candidate for you today. Or you may be faced with a pool of young candidates who haven't yet built an extensive work portfolio. With behavioral interviewing, you can generate meaningful discussions that can help you predict whether those candidates can deliver on the jobs you are working to fill. And when hourly job seekers don't have experience that specifically matches the jobs you're hiring for, this method is even more helpful.

Follow the law when interviewing ∎

Employment laws are specific about what you can and can't ask during an interview—with a goal of building consistent and fair practices for individuals seeking work today. As you prepare to interview candidates for your job, be sure you understand what you are able to legally ask during an interview. In general, employment laws prevent you from asking direct questions about your candidates':

- Nationality
- Religion
- Age
- Marital and family status
- Gender
- Health and physical abilities

However, you can ask specific questions related to those topics, to ensure you are meeting your other employment obligations. For example, you may not ask what country your candidates call home, but you can ask whether they are legally authorized to work in the United States and request supporting documentation. You can't ask whether candidates have children and daycare, but you can ask whether they are available to work specific shifts. And while you can't ask what religion job seekers follow, you can inquire as to whether they're available to work specific days of the week.

If you have questions about interviewing practices, we encourage you to contact your legal counsel.

Use the application and job seeker profile as a guide — not a blueprint — for finding right-fit employees.

What candidates tell you about their skills and experiences when applying for the job should help drive your interviews and shape the questions you plan to ask.

"The information is there," Riggs says. "It's just a matter of taking the time to review the application and asking the right questions."

Since hourly workers often don't have formal resumés, they may not be versed at telling their work or career stories in the same way as salaried workers. When coming up with interview questions, you need to look between the lines for clues about the experiences and past performance that will guide you in deciding whether to hire those candidates. When you are looking at an hourly candidate pool that can span from age 16 to 70, you need to be adaptable — but still consistent — in your interviewing style. Many younger candidates, for example, aren't practiced or prepared for a one-on-one interview, but that doesn't mean they won't make superstar hourly workers.

"There's not one size that fits all in the selection or interview process," say People Report's Doolin.

A set of common, consistently asked questions can help you gain a baseline of responses to use in weighing your hiring decisions. Within the hourly segment, where many candidates are still fresh in their work experience, Mel Kleiman believes that one of the most important questions to ask candidates is about the first job they got paid for — and what they learned along the way, including their interactions with their boss and colleagues.

"You can build the entire interview out of that one particular question," says Kleiman, founder of Humetrics, which provides best-practice research, tools and resources to companies looking to optimize their recruiting and hiring practices.

"You're looking for attitude," Kleiman says. "You want hourly workers who are dependable, honest and committed to your job, and you can train them to deliver your service in the way that reflects your culture."

Kleiman compares the recruiting and hiring process to preparing for a trip to the grocery store. The most frequent missteps people make when shopping are going hungry and without a list—it's too tempting to take the first things you see, which might not be what you want at a price you can afford, he cautions. "The biggest mistake people make in recruiting is that they haven't defined the target. What are you really looking for? How do you find it?"

And once that target is defined, you can ask truly meaningful questions and get creative with your interviews.

Are you looking for someone who can open your business at 4 a.m. every morning? Then arrange for the candidates to meet you exactly at that moment for their interviews, Kleiman advises. You want to know if they're responsible and trustworthy, so give them the chance to prove that. If the candidates don't show up, you've received your answer much more cheaply than finding out later they won't be there to open the business.

Connect with culture.

So you've found hourly candidates who can work the hours you want, with the skills you demand, at the pay rate you're offering. Before you sign them up, see if they can pass another, potentially more important test. Specifically, are they a great culture fit for your company?

Frame questions around the values that you and your frontline workers embrace to ensure an otherwise stellar hourly candidate passes this vital test. Does the candidate thrive in the type of collaborative environment that you've fostered on your front lines and behind the counter? Does the hourly job seeker have the interpersonal acumen to strike up the type of rapport that represents your customer service signature? Be sure to screen your candidates for these important criteria in addition to matching their skills and experience to the position you're seeking to fill. Don't trust yourself to gauge this culture match all by yourself; be sure to bring in a group of the applicant's would-be peers to chat and interact. A new worker who fails your culture test can be much more detrimental to the overall work environment than one without the basic required hard-skill competencies.

Developing interview questions from an hourly job seeker profile or application

What they tell you	What you should ask
Student government president	What was the biggest issue facing your school this year and what did you do as a student leader? What was the outcome?
Retail clerk	Tell me about the toughest customer service challenge you faced. How did you handle it?
Hotel housekeeper	What was the toughest cleaning assignment you have encountered? What did you do? Were you able to keep on your schedule for the day?

– SnagAJob.com

Not quite sure if this candidate is the right fit? Invite the applicant to try out the job—it's a win-win for both of you.

While interviews provide for one-on-one discussion that gives you insight into how the candidate might perform on the job, we all know that candidates (and even hiring managers) put on their best game face during that situation. Consider whether a job tryout could generate the extra information you need to make a qualified hire.

Starbucks is testing a Virtual Job Tryout® for individuals seeking retail management positions. The Virtual Job Tryout was developed by Shaker Consulting Group, an external vendor. Shaker worked closely with Starbucks to create an engaging experience for these candidates at the earliest contact point, while also finding a way to single out the strongest potential talent, said Gretchen Frampton, Starbucks program manager for assessments.

HIRE STANDARDS

Making Your Hiring Choice

Every hiring manager must weigh a variety of factors in determining whether to extend job offers to the candidates they interview. The Society for Human Resource Management asked HR professionals to rate different attributes in their hiring decisions. Among those earning the top spots for either "very influential" or "influential" were:

Interview Performance
95%

Professionalism in Interactions
95%

Years of Relevant Work Experience
90%

Fit with Company Culture
89%

Relevant Certifications
82%

Background Check
79%

– SHRM¹

The Virtual Job Tryout combines state-of-the-art psychometrics with an interactive, informative and company-branded candidate experience. Elements of the job are recreated in an on-line environment, providing the candidate a "test drive" of day-to-day work demands. Candidates complete five experiences in which they demonstrate critical thinking and problem-solving skills and give insight to work style preferences and work history. The tool provides a solid way to assess how a candidate with or without prior retail experience could succeed in the Starbucks environment.

The long-term goal of the Virtual Job Tryout is to improve performance by making the right initial hires. Validation analysis conducted with Starbucks partners (as Starbucks employees are called), demonstrated that Starbucks could see a significant improvement in business results by using the Virtual Job Tryout to identify, and stop hiring, applicants that perform in the bottom 20%.

"We aren't only hiring better candidates, but we are getting more and better information about all candidates," Frampton said. Starbucks uses that information to continuously monitor its return on investment, as they track the quality of hires to business results.

You're not just interviewing candidates—they're also interviewing you.

Now that we've shared some best practices for filtering and panning for golden candidates, it's time for you to woo these eager job seekers you're interviewing.

The interview experience should offer a window into your workplace. Paint a realistic picture for hourly candidates of the job they are pursuing, and make sure you're engaged when doing so.

Candidates know when they are your priority. When your candidates arrive for their interview, be ready. Hourly workers may have made arrangements for child care or made other accommodations to get to your business. Make sure they know that they have your attention throughout the interview. Let someone else answer your phone and designate a team member to handle immediate issues. You need to give your candidates your uninterrupted time to ask and answer hiring questions.

Don't forget to reserve time in your interview plan to review:

- Overall company mission and responsibilities for this job
- Pay for the position
- Benefits and workplace perks, including uniforms, if applicable
- Workplace expectations

"Remember, you only have one time to make a first impression," says Humetrics founder Kleiman. "That applicant is interviewing you just as much as they are being interviewed." Within a structured recruiting and selection process, all hiring managers can tap into a common set of questions that help them understand how those candidates will perform within the company's culture.

One more thing: The hiring manager shouldn't be alone in the interviewing process. The most important thing for your company at this point is to provide a window into your company culture and what you do. While your hiring manager can talk about your organization and the job, the companies that do best at hiring the right hourly workers expand the interview process to involve your current employees.

Why? Candidates always put their best face on when meeting with hiring managers, and you get more honest insight into potential employees' attitudes and discipline as they interact with people they will be working with on the front lines.

> "We aren't only hiring better candidates, but we are getting more and better information about all candidates."
>
> – Gretchen Frampton, Starbucks' program manager for assessments

Before you put on your job-selling hat, put yourself in the job seekers' sneakers.

Have you tried to get an hourly job at your company lately? You get a different perspective on your interview and hiring process by putting yourself in the candidate's shoes.

In December 2003, professor Jerry Newman left the classroom at the State University of New York at Buffalo, where he's a SUNY Distinguished Professor and noted compensation expert, to work at a handful of quick-serve restaurants. He detailed his 14-month experiment in *My Secret Life on the McJob: Lessons from Behind the Counter Guaranteed to Supersize Any Management Style*, published in 2007.

One of the most important lessons he learned is that "too often, the recruiting process is treated in isolation," he said in a recent conversation. That comes in direct contrast to companies, particularly in this industry, that are looking for people who must step into an integrated organization and its culture to deliver on the brand promise to customers. "These things need to be looked at together," added Newman. "What are you trying to accomplish as a whole? You need to understand who you are and your culture."

During his quick-service restaurant career, Newman worked at eight different concept stores. Managers at five of those companies spent less than five minutes interviewing him before offering him a job. And those interviewers all asked him the same trio of basic questions:

- Was he legally authorized to work in the United States?
- Did you have reliable transportation?
- What shifts could he work?

He quickly learned to note that he was available between 11 a.m.-3 p.m. to work the busiest time, the lunch shift. "That was a very popular answer," he said.

However, none of those managers took the time to find out if he really was the right person to step in with their current mix of employees. At a different restaurant, the manager asked if he smoked, knowing that a common bonding experience for that staff was the smoke break.

"Too often the recruiting process is treated in isolation."

– Jerry Newman, professor, State University of New York at Buffalo

"Hiring for the fit is an important factor in the overall selection," he said. "The more time that they spent in the interview, the better I later thought of what my manager was doing."

Newman also saw some positive interviewing strategies at the field level. Many managers arranged for on-site interviews in the late afternoon, before the final evening rush. At one local quick-service restaurant, Newman was interviewed by an 18-year-old manager following a standard set of behavioral interview questions. Although "he was going through the motions, he wasn't particularly well-prepared for it," said Newman, noting that the young manager did augment the discussion with information about what he would do on the job if hired.

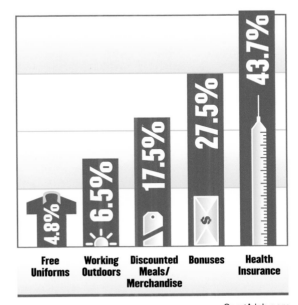

What benefits attract hourly workers?

- Free Uniforms: 4.8%
- Working Outdoors: 6.5%
- Discounted Meals/Merchandise: 17.5%
- Bonuses: 27.5%
- Health Insurance: 43.7%

– SnagAJob.com

When he interviewed at a different QSR location down the street, he met with a seasoned manager who knew exactly what she wanted: a person who knew when it was time to work and could also have fun on the job. She asked Newman—who is closer to retirement than starting a front-line hourly career—very targeted questions, including whether he viewed the job with dignity and what he would do if one of his students saw him behind the counter. Newman answered truthfully and got the job because he fit the exact characteristics that the manager needed in her newest employee.

This personalized, workplace culture-focused interview was in great contrast to the previous paint-by-numbers experience. And it's a model you should strive for.

"I don't think it is an unattainable goal," he said. "It's exactly what we need to be paying attention to."

Pulling the trigger

Here are some best practices for making hourly hiring happen without a hitch:

1. Do it quickly: We've mentioned multiple times throughout these chapters just how important speed is for hourly job seekers. And we'll say it again: Applicants expect some level of response within 48 hours of submitting their application.

2. Confirm schedule and obligations: Has the applicant started school or lost access to a car since he or she applied? Be sure to probe for this info before making the offer.

3. Schedule the first shift then and there: You already have the new hire's attention, so be sure to set up your first meeting, whether it's a training session, an actual shift or an information-gathering session. And relay all pertinent details, from where to park to what to wear.

4. Be ready to negotiate: If your starting wage isn't negotiable, be sure to say that. And if an applicant still isn't biting on your offer, be sure to mention all the additional perks you offer, such as an employee discount and medical benefits.

5. Respond to everyone: There's a solid chance all applicants—including the ones you reject—are also your patrons. Be sure to inform applicants not making the cut that you're passing on them. This will also save your frontline workers the hassle of having to perform this duty on the fly during the workday.

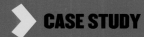

Oakwood Worldwide: Elevating Your Interview IQ

OPPORTUNITY: The Internet has opened up a broader, more qualified applicant pool than most employers have ever seen, but hourly workers are perishable. "They are in the market because they need a job," said Kymberly Garrett, director of talent acquisition at Oakwood Worldwide. "You need to treat them with more urgency." For Oakwood Worldwide, the leading provider of temporary corporate housing, that means connecting quickly with the right candidates and creating the right interview environment to take immediate action.

SOLUTION: By posting jobs online, Oakwood generates an ongoing pipeline of viable candidates. Online screening questions and tools provide an automated and immediate step for helping "to get to the gems" among a larger volume of applications, Garrett says. "You can be very creative and let your juices run very full to attract this type of worker," she notes. As they build up a pool of applicants, Oakwood creates a "red-carpet" interview experience in which candidates are welcomed to sites and treated like special guests. This includes giving away gift cards and other prizes to incentivize job seekers to attend one-day job fairs with hiring managers in local markets. Oakwood recruiters coach candidates in advance on what to expect and how to prepare and dress for their interview. "Our goal is to show we respect them, and to make them feel welcome and comfortable when they walk in the door," she says.

> "Our goal is to show we respect them, and to make them feel welcome and comfortable when they walk in the door."

RESULTS: Oakwood projects an annual hiring volume of 500 hourly workers, including drivers, housekeepers, leasing consultants and front-counter service representatives. During the local job fairs, Oakwood delivers on its promise to give job decisions on the spot. Garrett notes that applicants may have paid for a babysitter to come to that hiring event or even taken time off from another job, so they need to hear a decision immediately. The goal is to provide a high-touch experience for hourly candidates and create a one-on-one experience where recruiters can learn more about applicants. "We know and appreciate that their resumé isn't going to tell their story," which may provide practical information but not insight into their work ethic or success, Garrett says. But when given the opportunity to talk with a recruiter, candidates are "going to give me a conversation" —and a reason to make the right hire.

From the corner store to the corner office: making interviews matter

Before the interview, take time to think through the responsibilities for this role, so you are able to explain your expectations and to answer any questions from your candidates. Keep in mind that workforce dynamics are important no matter what the organization size, but staffing relationships are magnified in a small workplace. Craft your questions carefully so you can get insight that you can use to predict how that individual will fit in to your business.

You are probably building your hiring volumes at this point. As you talk with a growing pool of candidates, be sure that you are creating common lists of interview questions for the positions you hire for most. Use your understanding of your company's business to develop questions that enable candidates to show you how they would perform on the job.

You're likely hiring repeatedly for a core group of job roles. Now, more than ever, you need to ensure that your interview questions will generate candidates who reflect and reinforce your brand—or who you are as a company. With a growing number of hiring managers in multiple locations, it's important to continue to refine your common interview questions so you can enable your hiring team to identify qualified candidates who fit your corporate standards. If your business relies on field interviewing, take time regularly to review your local hiring managers to ensure they are using consistent and compliant standards.

Develop a common interview form

Take some of the work out of the interview process by developing a form that you can use each time to document candidate information, including how they respond to your questions. If you are using online or automated tools, such as an Applicant or Talent Management System, you probably have that feature available. The goal is to collect the same information about your different candidates so that you can make qualified, informed hiring decisions.

Here are some elements you should consider capturing:

Interview information form

Be sure to tell your staff—and even to indicate on the form itself—that interviewees should only transcribe the interview Q&A on this form, and for legal reasons, not add comments or other notes.

Candidate information
- Name
- Contact information

Assessments
- Performance on designated assessments or job screenings

Interview details and impressions
- Date/time of interview
- Was candidate prompt?
- Was candidate dressed appropriately and cleanly?

Interview questions and responses
- List common job-related questions and provide space for responses
- Include specific behavioral interview questions (situation, action, results)

Staff feedback
- Collect information from staff members who interviewed the candidate

Next steps
- Document required testing (e.g., drug screening, physical)
- Hiring decision

Follow the law with your questions

Remember that government regulations dictate what you can directly ask your potential hires. You need to provide a fair and consistent interview process. Consider how you can ask questions that get the information you need but still meet legal requirements. As always, consult with your legal counsel to review your interview practices in advance, to ensure that you are in compliance with the latest regulations.

Asking legal interview questions

Your Position: _____

Unable to ask:	What you need to know:	Suggested question:
Legal nationality	Eligible to work in United States?	
Religion	Available to work on Sunday?	
Family	Able to meet possible overtime demand?	

– SnagAJob.com

Sources

| Society for Human Resource Management, "Selection Criteria." Alexandria, Va.: June 15, 2003. <http://shrm.org/press/ntu_published/CMS_005942.asp#P-6_0>.

Notes

What are you doing to guarantee **your new hires will love it from day one?**

Everyone is "on" during the job interview—smiling, choosing words carefully and often looking to please.

But when your new workers punch the clock for the first time, you're both interacting in a more disarming setting. And you're both on the clock. Seize the moment and make their first day a positive experience. You have the tools and resources to create an environment that enables your new hires to be their best on the job.

The biggest mistake you can make at this time is failing to follow through. You have already invested significant time and money in seeking and interviewing new hourly workers. Your focus for your new hires' first day should be on taking care of logistical issues, such as tax paperwork and handing out uniforms, as well as immersing them in your culture. The most important thing that you can give your new hire on the first day is uninterrupted time. You don't need to clear your whole day—and you can't be expected to—but you need to demonstrate to your hourly workers that you value their commitment to your team.

"If the general manager takes the time to conduct the orientation experience personally, there is a tremendous increase later in the tenure of that employee," says Joni Thomas Doolin, founder and CEO of People Report. "When you talk to companies or managers who are really successful in retaining a talented workforce, some of it is as simple as taking time."

Be ready to put your new hires to work immediately.

Think long-term: Build strategies to support your newest hourly workers on their first day, in their first week and in their first month.

Support your hourly workers in gaining new skills and talents to grow with your business.

> ### When it comes to making a solid first impression, **you're both on the clock.**

How well you take care of your new employees during that first day or week directly translates into how quickly they build their productivity on the job—and ultimately whether they decide to stay with your company. With the turnover rate in hourly industries exceeding 100 percent, this is your first toehold into achieving greater retention with new hires.

You should take time to plot out a three-step strategy that ensures long-term success for you and your new hire:

Day One: Greet them warmly and build an orientation experience that introduces them to their new teammates and outlines what they need to do to succeed at that job. Be engaging and encourage the new hires to ask questions. On the more practical side, make sure they have a place to store their jacket or purse, receive a clean uniform (if appropriate) and take care of any outstanding employment paperwork. Consider pairing them up with a job buddy to shadow who will show them the ropes. This job buddy should also be the go-to person if questions and problems arise. All employees remember their first day on the job; will you make this a positive memory?

Week One: Arrange time for your new hires to meet people outside of their immediate area of responsibility and learn about other areas of your business. Engage them in any culture-building efforts you have, such as a workplace intranet.

Month One: Plan for a check-in at the 30-day mark, whether by the local hiring manager or another supervisor. During this initial performance review, provide solid examples of excellence on the job and provide strategies, such as targeted training, to address opportunities for improvement. Review your orientation checklist and act on any outstanding items. After this first month, be sure to include additional periodic reviews, skill refreshers and training sessions.

These first few days and weeks are when you invest most significantly in training new hires. Just as critical, this is the time when you need to oversee how your current employees engage with their newest colleagues. Lead by example in bringing your company culture to life.

On-boarding motto: Be thoughtful and consistent. Or be ready to do it again and again.

Consider that when an hourly worker starts a new job, that individual may be coming to a workplace with employees crossing four generations and representing different nationalities —all coming together to present language and other cultural barriers. The job experiences and academic backgrounds of the current workforce may be just as diverse. The manager on duty is tasked with building a work environment that motivates and inspires all employees to deliver their best performance.

How well that newest hire does starts and ends the moment that person walks in the door.

"The good managers want to send the right message on the first day," says T.J. Schier, president and founder of Incentivize Solutions, which provides training and motivational resources for today's workers. "If orientation is an afterthought, it just sends the wrong message to the employees. The intent is always there. But oftentimes, the reality of the situation takes over. That's really the beginnings of poor management and heavy turnover."

The author of "*Send Flowers to the Living! Rewards, Contests and Incentives to Build Employee Loyalty*," Schier understands the frontline challenges as owner of several Which Wich Superior Sandwiches franchises around Dallas and Houston.

Make sure new hires understand why you are giving them this time right now, he says. Starting a new job can be intimidating, and you don't want new employees to think they're a burden or that you don't have time for them. New hires need to know and believe that the time you spend with them is the most important duty you could be performing.

"This session should be about the 'whys.' 'Why do we do this?' 'Why do we do that?'" Schier adds. "It's not just a rules session. It's about how to be successful with our company and how to make money."

Jerry Newman witnessed this first-hand when he took jobs at several quick-service restaurants. Receiving quality one-on-one time with the restaurant manager made a tremendous difference.

"The best stores did that; the worst stores didn't," says Newman, professor at the State University of New York at Buffalo. The more time invested by the manager, the lower the turnover and the higher the level of engagement among the current workers, he adds.

As demonstrated across the recruiting and hiring cycle, putting a common orientation plan in place streamlines your work requirements with each new hire. Your goal is to create a welcome program that explains the business, where those new employees fit in, what is expected of them and why they're so important to the business. Your initial focus at orientation should be on the big picture; then you can move into the functional training that prepares employees for the unique elements of their job.

"On-boarding helps to instill a comfort level for the employee from day one," Schier says. "It gives the employees confidence and tells them where to go if they have questions. It eases all of the fears and concerns for the employees."

Don't overlook what a great on-boarding experience means for you either. Dedicating the time and attention upfront to readying your new hire for the job means you'll spend less time later on recruiting for and training that same position again. You'll also earn the respect of your new hires by carving out this quality time and building rapport.

Training Matters

The Great Place to Work Institute reports that the companies ranked as the best places to work in the country spend the following time and money training their employees:

Medium Companies	Top 25	Top 10	Top 5
Percent of Annual Budget Allocated to Training	3%	3%	4%
Average Hours Per Year Allocated to Training	49 hours	57 hours	74 hours

– The Great Place to Work Institute[1]

Building a culture of inclusion doesn't just include your new hires. Get your superstar employees in the mix.

There are two roles you can assign your employees to help with some of the on-boarding heavy-lifting:

Champion: Choose a leader who takes responsibility for making sure your new hire gets to know everyone at the workplace and knows where to come if and when questions come up on the job. This person needs to step in and be an advocate who can effectively integrate your new hires into the team. Be sure to pay your champions a "spiff," a spot bonus that shows your gratitude for the role they've played in on-boarding.

Ally: This ally can help your new hire learn more about how the team works, while keeping your other employees focused on their primary responsibilities. Make sure this connection starts on the first day, but the assignment can be phased out within about a month. Whether your employees are assisting with interviews or serving as job buddies, always be proactive in instructing them the right and acceptable way to conduct themselves, rather than having to un-teach bad habits.

While these strategies may be specifically targeted to help orient new team members, you are also building relationships that will drive your employees' long-term success.

THE WELCOME NEVER ENDS

Effective On-Boarding

According to the Aberdeen Group, a Boston-based provider of fact-based research and market intelligence, new employees, "often feel that the attention they received during the pre-hire stages is abandoned once they are on board." Ninety percent of companies believe that workers decide whether or not to stay within the first six months on the job.

An on-boarding strategy is one way to address this concern. The Aberdeen Group cites other top pressures that are leading companies to develop more formal on-boarding programs—pressures that become benefits of successful on-boarding when executed correctly.

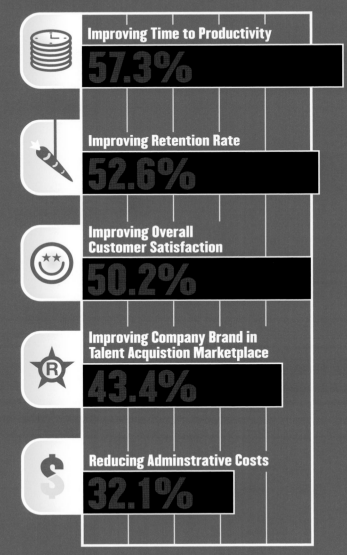

Improving Time to Productivity
57.3%

Improving Retention Rate
52.6%

Improving Overall Customer Satisfaction
50.2%

Improving Company Brand in Talent Acquistion Marketplace
43.4%

Reducing Adminstrative Costs
32.1%

– Aberdeen Group"

Don't assume that your new hires know what you want them to do—
and how you want it done.

You want your employees doing the job they were hired to do as soon as possible. Getting to know your business and your people should be your focus for new hourly workers during orientation; training should get them to know what you expect them to do every day. In many large companies, training may happen at a corporate level under the HR team. In the realities of the front-line or operations hourly worker, training is delegated to the local managers.

With annual training in the quick-service restaurant business alone topping $1,630 per employee, costs add up quickly.[III] Those investments underscore how critical the selection process serves in identifying right-fit employees who will stay with your company. Much of the hourly training investment is made early in that new hire's tenure, so retention is valuable in ensuring you recoup those training dollars in your business's profit column.

 **With the right bells, whistles and buttons, technology can
fast track on-boarding.**

Technology can provide a foundation for capturing and delivering key information across the on-boarding and training process. You can start by delivering required employment forms online, where employees can go to access tax forms, identification forms and benefits enrollment, if applicable. Some companies may enable electronic submission of paperwork, while you still need to do in-person verification of identity and right-to-work documents.

Technology also opens up fresh ways to introduce your business and show new workers how to master the right behaviors and job skills. For example, T.J. Schier's company, Incentivize Solutions, helps businesses in developing iPod tours of the workplace. He compares it to the headphone guided tours available in museums. The iPod sessions walk new hires through the location, telling them where to find things and what the business does at different stations. Your new employees can take the tour at their own pace and revisit topics at their leisure, while they may be hesitant to ask about things they don't understand. That includes reinforcing small touches required to meet brand standards, such as folding T-shirts in a specific way for retail displays. After completing these tours, new hires now have a solid business foundation from which to direct their specific questions. They might have been embarrassed to simply ask where the freezer is located, but after completing a do-it-yourself tour, they can ask about the optimal temperature for storing frozen beef patties.

In "*My Secret Life on the McJob*," Jerry Newman notes that the best training programs had the same ingredients: a focus on communicating the most important worker behaviors with a careful eye on making sure "that these behaviors were being learned and demonstrated accurately."[IV]

Adds People Report's Joni Thomas Doolin: "If an employee isn't confident in the job, it's going to show. You need to give them the skills to go out and take care of business, particularly in customer-facing roles."

Your employees make money for you. Are you giving them a piece of the action?

While every business should set basic job expectations for every role and every employee, incentives add value by recognizing the performers who go above and beyond those expectations, Schier suggests. In his Which Wich stores, he knows his basic business costs don't change, starting with what he has to spend on food.

"As a business owner, I always want to get my results first," Schier says. But by running a viable business, which relies on strong employee contributions, he can then enable his employees to share in those results.

The key to that is making sure that employees understand what you do and how you make money. Part of that lesson is explaining to them where their work fits into the bigger picture. "The more your employees know about your business, the more they can help your business," Schier says.

Time is money, but just how much? ▪

Let's pull some hypotheticals together and scope out just how much money a frontline manager could save by following on-boarding best practices. In Scenario I, a manager is stubbornly sticking to his or her old ways of recruiting by neglecting to spend quality one-on-one time with new hires. However, Scenario II shows an enlightened manager open to doing things a bit differently. This manager uses more time—and time costs money—but does it pay for itself in the end? Let's take a look:

▪ SCENARIO I

$25	Managerial hourly wage
3 hrs	Average time spent on-boarding new hire
20	Total employees
X 1.0	100 percent turnover rate

$1,500

▪ SCENARIO II

$25	Managerial hourly wage
5 hrs	Average time spent on-boarding new hire
20	Total employees
X 0.5	50 percent turnover rate

$1,250

In Scenario II, you'll see that by increasing the time you spend on-boarding by just a few hours, you start saving money within the first 12 months of the trade-off. Sure, $250 in savings may not seem like a lot, but play out this scenario another year, and you're making 10 hires instead of an additional 20, resulting in exponential savings.

Prevent information overload

Be wary of overloading your new employee with too much information on the first day—and be open to drawing a line between on-boarding and training.

If you're filling a quick-serve restaurant shift and your new hire worked at the competitor across the street, you may be able to plug that new worker right into your team rather seamlessly. If, however, you are hiring a retail clerk, you may want to invest more time up-front in explaining your business and what you do.

Martin Riggs suggests that businesses hold off on official training until the second day. Spend that initial day instead on helping new workers understand your culture and philosophy. If your critical focus is on service, then provide examples of key service and explain your principles—don't jump right into how to ring up an order.

"That's a lot of pressure to put on a new person," Riggs says. "It should be a stress-free day for the new employees."

Incentives such as spot bonuses, customer service awards and paid time off—the most desired incentive—provide you with a resource for getting strong talent to stay late or cover shifts for sick employees. They also can be used to reward employees for doing something extraordinary to take care of your customer. Again, though, the limit is that incentives reinforce what your best workers already are doing. "Incentives can't get the wrong person to do the right thing," he says.

"The most effective incentive is the one the employee wants," Schier says. Therefore, the best thing for a manager to do is to find out what the employees want—for example, gift cards or more money. For a manager to pick what they want as an incentive and think it will work is typical, but not effective.

Some effective incentives include: music download cards, ringtone download cards, electronics gift cards, gas cards, movie passes and "experience certificates" (skiing, amusement parks, spa, etc.).

"I have found that if you have employees who are sending money home to another country, that money is far more effective than gift cards, so make sure you know your employees and what motivates them," Schier says.

Have you started looking for your next managerial candidate?
You may already have the best hires under your roof.

One thing is constant in the employment industry: People change jobs. Businesses are constantly in the recruiting process. However, don't automatically post a job listing externally for the latest managerial position that you need to fill, such as a shift supervisor or assistant manager. Start by looking internally at your current staff and determine whether you could offer the role to one of your top hourly workers. You can provide career paths for your current employees—a critical strategy in retaining top workers.

Managing an hourly workforce includes planning for their future with your company. While some employees may want to stay on the morning shift, which allows them to work while their children are in school, others may very well be looking to move into management roles. In fact, according to a SnagAJob.com survey of nearly 2,000 Americans between the age of 18 and 29, 40 percent of those in this demographic see themselves as career hourly workers, or "new collar workers." There are countless stories about entry-level, new collar workers joining a business and quickly climbing the ladder of responsibility, ultimately becoming supervisors, managers, and even franchise owners and beyond.

The important thing is to create a framework for regular discussions with your people. Start by providing feedback about ways your workers are contributing to your business's success. You should also review opportunities for improvement, which may include recommending targeted training sessions to master necessary skills. These performance reviews keep you engaged with your employees and help you understand how their long-term goals align with yours.

"You can't let people wait for six months to learn how they are doing. That needs to be an ongoing process," says People Report's Doolin, noting that hourly workers are often delivering on their key responsibilities within their first days. "People need you to communicate to them about their work."

The hourly workforce is different. Workers in salaried roles often are given six months to learn the business and launch their action plan before managers sit down for a formal performance assessment. In many cases, six months is the full tenure for an hourly worker —unless their managers are regularly connecting with them.

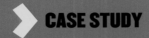

Veolia Transportation: Retaining Momentum

OPPORTUNITY: Veolia Transportation recognized that the recruitment market for top hourly workers was challenging. By the time the private transit company identified candidates for interviews, many had already taken other jobs, says Pat Gerace, director of recruiting and a 17-year HR veteran. Veolia's market research showed that its targeted talent pool often committed one day specifically for getting a job, with those hourly candidates directly investing in child care and transportation costs while they searched. "They would go to different places until someone said 'You're hired,'" Gerace says. "They need to get a job that day. Looking for a job can be a financial burden for them."

> "We really turned a corner in how we operate, so that we could make conditional hires immediately."

SOLUTION: Veolia reinvented its recruiting strategy to support both on-the-spot hiring and direct training placement. The company's efforts began with streamlining its process for requiring pre-employment screens, including criminal background and drug tests, along with driving record reviews and physical exams for applicable positions. Recruiters also took their employment message into the community, where potential candidates could easily engage with Veolia. That outreach included community job fairs, GED and ESL classes and church events. There Veolia representatives outlined career opportunities, beginning with training that specifically prepares new hires for success and supports the company's culture of safety from the start.

RESULTS: Today Veolia Transportation has more than 17,000 employees and operates 150 contracts for cities and transit authorities in the United States and Canada. New hires, including drivers and maintenance workers, can be on the payroll within five days now, as Veolia hires directly to fill scheduled training classes. "We really turned the corner in how we operate, so that we could make conditional hires immediately," says Gerace, reflecting on Veolia's refinements in hiring top hourly workers. "Success in high-volume recruiting really needs to be respectful and mindful of those differences."

From the corner store to the corner office: sealing the deal and details

You may be deeply ingrained in the day-to-day challenges of running a small business. Pull your head up and assess how you welcome new employees and prepare them for the tasks and responsibilities of their new jobs. Do you do little more than greet them at the door and put them to work, hoping they'll learn by osmosis? Build a plan that reflects what they need to know and how to connect them with their co-workers and other resources to achieve their potential.

Do you have on-boarding milestones in place to track and assess your employees over their first few weeks and beyond? If not, it's time to add these milestones before your business becomes too big to easily implement them.

Take a hard look at the ROI from both your on-boarding and training investments. You are hiring significant volumes each year, so make sure you are applying best practices to get synergies across the organization. You should have demonstrated repeatable processes that are streamlined for both your hiring managers and your new employees. At the same time, keep your eyes on your corporate vision for the next year and ensure you refine your on-boarding and training programs so that your newest workers are positioned with the job skills to deliver on that strategy.

1. Plan a consistent on-boarding experience

Making new hires feel welcome from the moment they walk in your door goes a long way in making them happy, content, loyal and productive workers. No matter what other demands you are facing, reserve time in your schedule to greet them, introduce them to their co-workers and take care of any lingering employment tasks. Plan out your new hires' first days or weeks to continue the on-boarding process so they get an opportunity to meet people in other areas and understand the big picture of what your organization does every day.

2. Build a training program that grows with your workers

Your immediate responsibility is to prepare your hourly workers to step into their new roles and responsibilities successfully. So the initial training should focus precisely on helping them master those skills. However, to build engagement and retention, you need to be thinking forward to your hourly employees' future with your business, then have a training strategy that allows them to grow with your company. Keeping your current employees and training them for other responsibilities is healthier for your bottom line than going back to the recruiting stage.

3. Calculate what training means to you

As the adage goes, you need to spend money to make money. Training is a perfect example of how you can turn an investment into profit, if you think wisely up front about where you're putting those dollars.

Workforce Management, through its workforce.com site, outlines a four-step process for determining the benefits of the investment you make in training. It's easy to determine what you're spending and where that money is going, but think strategically to identify where you're making gains that improve your bottom line.

1. Understanding training costs & benefits

	What it includes	What it means to your business
Calculate the Cost of Training	• Training materials • Trainer fees • AV costs • Production downtime, while your hourly workers are off the job • Location costs	*Where are you spending your training dollars?*
Determine the Potential Savings Generated	• Fewer errors • Reduced customer turnover • Better equipment operation • Increased revenue collection • Higher morale and engagement	*Where do you see savings generated by your training investments?*
Calculate the Potential Savings	• Current level of performance and costs • Target outcomes to be achieved by training • Calculate potential savings and timeframe	*What can you expect to achieve by launching a specific training initiative?*
Compare Costs to Savings	• Compare figures to frame business case for training	*Will training costs justify expected savings and additional revenue?*

2. Training schedule by role

Time	What you need to do for your new hire	What your company offers
First Day	• Technology training (cash register, computer log-ins, etc.) • Customer service standards (how to greet customers, create invoices, etc.) • Basic job skills (key job performance, from outlining travel route for drivers to explaining how to work on-site equipment)	
First Week	• Cross-training for any roles that your new hire might be asked to step into	
First Month	• Understand what your employee is seeking in the long term with your company; present development opportunities that help them move toward those goals (management training, etc.)	
Every 6 Months	• Check in with that hire to gauge job performance and satisfaction • Look for opportunities that maximize any new skills developed	

3. On-boarding calendar

Time	Options	What can you do at your company?
First Day	• Welcome immediately • Complete final paperwork (make sure all documentation is complete before they start to work) • Review benefits (applicable holidays, health coverage, discount, etc.) • Introduce to key peers • Give tour of workplace and explain where to find things • Distribute uniform, etc. • Explain basic job responsibilities • Talk about why their job is so crucial to the business • Review company values, mission statement, etc. • Deliver initial training	
First Week	• Introduce new hire to key individuals they need to know across the business • Provide information about what the company does, e.g., direct them to corporate website, provide brochures, etc. • Show them how to find information they might need, e.g., company directory, equipment manuals, etc. • Review initial job performance and answer any questions about how to do the job	
First Month	• Sit down with your new hire and encourage them to ask any questions • Review job performance and identify next training opportunities • Review potential career paths	

Sources

I   Great Place to Work Institute, Inc. 2008 Best Medium Company to Work for in America list. 2008.

II   Aberdeen Group. "All Aboard: Effective Onboarding Strategies and Techniques." Boston. November 2007.

III   People Report. "New Economy Workforce Reality in a Bricks & Mortar World." Dallas, Texas. 2008. 21.

IV   Newman, Jerry: *My Secret Life on the McJob: Lessons from Behind the Counter Guaranteed to Supersize Any Management Style*. New York: McGraw Hill. 2007. 145.

V   Workforce Management (workforce.com). "TOOL: Calculate the Cost and Benefits of Training." August 2008. <http://www.workforce.com/section/11/article/23/95/44.html>.

Notes

CHAPTER 9

Taking It to the Next Level

Get targeted. Get measured. **And get ready to see your bottom line soar.**

Do you know what success means to you? Whether you are hiring one new employee at a given time or are constantly digging into your pipeline to keep your front-line ranks filled, you need to understand what is important to you—then ensure your recruitment strategies are supporting your goals.

Recruiting and hiring the right employees is a fine craft, but the right tools and supporting resources can drive efficiencies in your business and help you make informed decisions. The smarter choices you make up front, the greater the returns you make on your:

Recruiting investment: You need to know precisely where your dollars are going and how that comes back to your business through the talent and people you hire.

Workforce development: When you hire right-fit employees for your business, you are making enhancements that stretch far beyond single roles. You are making strategic selections that build satisfaction across your ranks and engage all workers in remaining with your business for longer periods.

Overall bottom line: By hiring people with the specific talents and skills to succeed in your organization, you are hiring people who can quickly deliver efficiency and quality service to your customers.

Your own employment numbers—your key business metrics—tell your story. Once you understand what core pieces of information you need to gauge your success—such as your annual turnover rate—you can then leverage both proven and emerging strategies to drive the results you need for your company. Ultimately, only you can decide what is game-changing to your business.

Financial numbers are the end-game metrics for your business. Your employment numbers—which represent your people and their contributions—are the fuel that feeds your business to achieve these end-game results. You constantly need to reflect on the value that your hires deliver and where your analysis identifies gaps. You face many decisions in making your business thrive against increasing challenges; workforce analytics provide an

Identify your key metrics; then track and analyze these metrics to identify trends and opportunities.

Keep your eyes open on the recruiting frontier. New technologies are changing how today's workers—particularly younger generations—are engaging with employers and their peers.

Look for ongoing ways to refine both your strategies and tactics to deliver targeted results, such as new demographic segments.

objective framework for making the smartest choices that have the greatest impact on your long-term success. But if you try to sell best recruitment practices to C-level executives at your company without supporting the move with time and cost metrics, you'll get nowhere fast. And if you can't justify the value of integrating the best practices we've advocated in previous chapters, your training becomes inconsistent, and sooner than later your budgets get cut.

 ## Your people drive your success.

We know that a comprehensive recruitment strategy begins with knowing who to hire— and ends by confirming that you are delivering on those expectations.

The final step of your hourly recruitment transformation involves identifying what you really want to gain from an effective hiring strategy. Most of our clients tell us that lowering their hiring costs and reducing turnover are most important to them.

"There are different measures of success," says Steve Earl, director of marketing for Kronos' talent management division. "Workforce analytics is about getting great insight into your data so that you can make better decisions. In order to measure the data, you need to capture the right information up front so that you know the problem you're trying to solve."

Effective analysis, Earl notes, should be grounded in two areas:

Transactional: This is your pure numbers game. How many people are applying for your jobs? Where are they hearing about your jobs? Who are you hiring?

Productivity: You want to assess the quality of your hires by looking at their contributions to your business. How long is their service? How much are they selling? How were their customer satisfaction scores?

Hourly hiring is, in general, a large-volume business, providing a wealth of information if you have time to pore over your data. Increased use of technology across your people platform provides a range of information to access, from application volume on your Talent Management System to exit dates tracked in your payroll system. HR is a transaction-based function, so look for your range of data sources. The best analytical models look at the entire employment lifecycle.

Just as important, research your industry to determine benchmark metrics that give you an external measure of your performance. You can look for internal ways to make gains, but that industry perspective can reinforce if you're on track from the beginning.

Here's a quick and easy chart you can fill in to measure and benchmark your various recruitment and retention initiatives against your own historical performance—and against the competition:

Objective	What specifically are you trying to achieve?
Strategy	What's your roadmap for getting "there"?
Tactics	These are your strategies broken down into bite-size actionable items.
Measurement	How will you know when you've crossed the threshold of success?

On the surface, many things are easy to measure, such as identifying the primary channel from which candidates hear about your jobs. Your analytical tools enable you to drill down for value-added information, such as the main source that captures the people you actually hire. That data spotlight gives you an objective angle for where you should focus your marketing resources. For example, if 50 percent of applicants say they were attracted to your company because of the workplace picture you paint in your job postings, you might want to add even more about your culture through words, pictures, video and even worker testimonials.

Finally, be sure to give your business time. You can get an immediate measure of any metric, but you need to give any new tactic or enhancement time to have an impact. Plan to go back and look at your results about three to 12 months after strategic launches.

How to measure a metric

In the first chapter, we detailed the importance of understanding the financial impacts of your recruitment strategy, which provides a foundation for determining your healthy bottom line. We also walked you through a basic model for calculating your overall recruitment costs.

Now that we're circling back to see how new best practices and models can drive financial gains, you need to pinpoint specific metrics. That means recognizing the most valuable data points to leverage in assessing your performance in a specific recruitment metric. Let's look at potential information for two core recruitment metrics:

Cost-per-hire: Go back to your initial recruitment strategy calculation. Be sure you incorporate related new employee costs, such as training and uniforms. Then divide that total by the number of people you hired during the same timeframe as you spent that money.

Retention and turnover: On the surface, these seem quite similar. But remember, turnover is not always bad. That's because turnover has some elements you can't control, such as when employees move, return to college, etc. Retention is a far better measure of employee quality than annual turnover. This figure provides a good measure for the percentage of your workforce that is still around after 90, 120 or 180 days, Kronos' Earl advises.

Metrics and their meaning to you

Consider the following a menu of metrics at your disposal. Just like a restaurant menu, you're not going to order everything on it. Choose two or three sound metrics that really speak to your business.

Metric	Significance
Application-to-Hire Ratio	Ratios below 10:1 present staffing problems for location managers, and identify the need for additional sourcing activities at the local level.
New Hire Retention	Reflects on-boarding and training success. Can be an indicator of local managerial capability. Calls attention to local labor market dynamics.
Assessment Scores	A measure of average applicant quality by location. Lower scores indicate a need for more sourcing activity so hiring manager can select from higher quality candidate pool.
Referral Source	Identifies productivity of sourcing activities. Allows companies to conduct ROI calculations on newspaper ads, job boards and other sourcing activities.
Application Preference	Identifies whether most candidates prefer walk-in or online applications and has implications for advertising activities as well as application delivery.
Key Position Dynamics	Certain locations often have trouble filling positions key to business success, such as sales specialists. Identifying these challenges allows companies to develop targeted sourcing programs at the location level.[1]
Overtime	Are you understaffed to the point that you're paying hourly employees a higher wage to work overtime?
Time to Fill	Refers to total vacancy time of open positions.
WOTC	Are you receiving Work Opportunity Tax Credits for hiring workers in applicant compliance segments prone to a higher-than-average percentage of unemployment?
Percent of False Starts	Are employment offers rescinded due to failed drug or background test/checks?
Internal Referrals	Do current employees fill a pipeline of direct promotions?
Cost-per-Hire	Once you have a handle on these core stats, you'll be in a position to calculate this comprehensive metric.

▶ Your data analysis **should come with a two-way window.**

Looking back gives you insight into how you have performed over time; looking ahead shapes your forecasting to help make business decisions that align with evolving market conditions. Starbucks uses workforce analytics to support the recruiting process in two ways: to provide a 12-month operational window on expected employee or partner needs across the organization, and to frame a three-year strategic outlook, according to Lacey All, head of strategic workforce planning for the Seattle-based coffee company.

This internal picture doesn't stand alone. Starbucks' understanding of retail segments, demographic trends, business-level needs and illustrations of future needs help steer appropriate decision-making at all levels, from hourly through salaried hiring. Quarterly reports, providing a one-year outlook, are developed and shared based on sales and store growth, coupled with turnover and internal movements.

A common, steady base of information enables the company to better track and analyze employment patterns and practices over time, particularly as business and market conditions change in tandem. Ongoing discussion with the business enables the Talent Management team—including strategic workforce planning, global staffing and organizational design—to refine its people practices and workforce modeling. "Our active engagement in the business' strategic priorities ensures we are making better decisions that have a positive impact on the global organization," All noted.

The metrics that are important to Starbucks evolved based on what leaders saw as core factors in achieving business goals and long-term success. Fundamentally, Starbucks is in the business of people, coffee and creating the coffeehouse experience that inspires and nurtures the human spirit. To help gauge whether the global staffing team was finding the right people, the strategic workforce planning team sought out internally collected data that provides actionable information, including indicators such as partner engagement, customer loyalty and partner tenure which reflect growth and maturity with the company. They couple this data with key external factors, All said. "Together this helps us understand and have a rich picture of internal and external factors that impact the supply and demand of our workforce."

"You need to keep it basic in determining your own key indicators to measure," All said. "Keep it simple – look for things that you can track against and that measure your success in prioritized areas," she added, noting that it's easy to get caught in trying to monitor too many internal barometers when three to five key metrics can tell the complete story. "You need to get down to the few critical things that are important to your business."

Better data collection also opens opportunities for you to "slice and dice" your information to drive enhancements at local and regional hiring levels, adds Kronos' Earl. "The talent shortage can be very local and often varies by region or location," he says. Having the ability to zoom in on what is happening at a specific site location can enable you to track locally what is working (and what is not) in sourcing new talent—and then make adjustments at the site or region level.

"It allows corporate to get visibility into whom and how a region is hiring and to offer more tools to help the local hiring manager," he adds, noting that the recruitment team needs to analyze results both at a corporate and regional level in order to take appropriate actions in all areas. That may mean improving selection tools or tweaking an employee referral program. "There's no one answer because demographics and local constraints often dictate what is going on site by site, region by region, but feeding valuable site-level information back into your recruitment strategy will help address these varying localized issues."

Are you pushing toward new frontiers in your recruiting and employment practices?

Now that you have solid information about your performance, hone in on operational and marketing gaps—and look for ways to blow out the tactics that hit your mark.

After all, you'll never change your results if you never change what you're doing. The first important step is to look internally at how you are operating, including your targeted candidate pool and basic processes. Don't look at your business metrics and immediately latch on to the latest trend. You may find that the greatest potential for growth is refining your basic recruitment strategy:

1. Draw a bull's eye on who you want to hire: The hourly recruitment market ranges from teens to retired baby boomers. Trying to market your open positions to potentially four generations of workers may mean that you're not effectively getting your message out to any of them. Your workforce analysis enables you to pinpoint precisely the employee demographic that delivers for you.

Once you parcel out what defines your strongest workers—and understand their availability in your local hiring pool—consider how you market directly to those individuals. You may find that your job descriptions for younger workers need to promote a fun work environment and culture—while return-to-work moms want flexible hours. Seasonal workers may value an employee discount more than a high hourly wage. And boomers returning to the hourly job after working salaried careers might signal the need to promote workplace flexibility or part-time gigs.

2. Tailor your recruiting practices so you can beef up the ranks when needed: We all know that the fourth quarter is the busiest time for retailers, while warm-weather months mean outdoor businesses—such as landscaping companies and theme parks—need greater worker volumes. If you operate in an industry that has seasonal fluctuations, align your recruiting efforts to your busy times so that you deliver trained workers when you need them at the front line. You can fast-track seasonal hiring by keeping in occasional contact with the best of your former employees, and keep them interested in you by offering a year-long employee discount even if they're only working three months.

3. Make sure new locations are ready for business on the first day: Many of you know how challenging it can be just to find one strong new hire. Securing the full complement of hires for a new store or restaurant can be daunting, but specialized resources can support you in quickly making volumes of qualified hires.

For example, staffing support company Self Opportunity specializes in providing open houses, career fairs and onsite tactics that streamline short-term, high-volume hiring. Their strategies are designed to create "buzz in a community. You're going to get an onslaught of applications," says Sean Self, president of Self Opportunity.

Managing complete hiring for a new location can be daunting for a single recruiter due to the sheer time and application review required. A company such as Self Opportunity can step in with a targeted hiring fair marketed both externally and to internal applicant pools. The partner can collect resumés, provide telephone resources and create a single-day event in which local hiring managers can meet with qualified candidates, he says. The external partner essentially takes over the exhaustive behind-the-scenes legwork, leaving final interviewing and hiring in your hands.

Most importantly, every element of the marketing effort reflects your company's brand and culture. "We want those people to be able to imagine themselves in your environment," Self says.

Another strategy is to tap into local career fairs, where recruitment partners promote hourly jobs across industry sections. The firms leverage their internal applicant databases to invite candidates with similar employment preferences. Participants have the opportunity to talk with different employers in different businesses. The drawback is that "everyone is obviously bidding on the same candidate," Self notes.

Hang ten on the technological wave and make a splash with potential hourly workers.

In recent years, we have witnessed the transformation of the job search process with new technology. We at SnagAJob.com are perfect proof that hourly workers not only are becoming more comfortable with using the Internet in their quest for new jobs, but they're also more dependent on it.

"People are going to Google right from the start when they go looking for a job," says Lori Charest, vice president for new media strategy at Waltham, Mass.-based TMP Worldwide Advertising & Communications, which has an employment marketing division. The Internet and related technology should be part of any effective strategy today—while keeping an eye looking forward to leverage emerging opportunities when they make sense for your organization, she adds.

Even as technology creates immediate communication, job seekers aren't ready to give up the face-to-face interaction completely, Charest says. Online features and functions can support both engagement and streamlined operations. "As more and more companies determine the right way to take their messaging online, they still need to be smart about where they spend their money as well."

Again, examine your hiring and business numbers to guide you in making choices that can change up your game:

More than words make a difference. One way that hourly workers explore potential employers is by exploring your corporate website. As your business grows and your recruiting demands intensify, assess whether you are using your site to tell the full story about why your company is a great place to work.

And if a picture, as they say, is worth a thousand words, imagine the exponential value that comes with a day-in-the-life workplace video. Seek out your top talent and showcase their success stories—literally in their own words—in online video. The latest research from Borrell Associates reinforces that "video is the hottest new tool for employers."[ii] This is especially true for teens and 20-somethings; SnagAJob.com research shows that 16 to-24-year-old hourly job seekers value pictures and video in their job description over wage details and quick readability.

LIGHTS. CAMERA. HIRE!

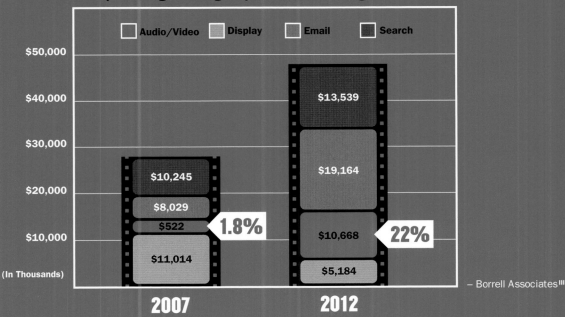

Online Ad Spending for Video (2007/2012)

Total percentage of budget spent on video listings

- Audio/Video
- Display
- Email
- Search

$50,000

$40,000 — $13,539

$30,000 — $19,164

$20,000 — $10,245

$8,029

$522 — **1.8%** — $10,668 — **22%**

$10,000 — $11,014 — $5,184

(In Thousands)

2007   **2012**

– Borrell Associates[III]

You also need to make sure your words matter. The standard way to capture job seekers when they are surfing the web for job leads is through Search Engine Optimization. As new employees apply or join your team, take time to capture how they specifically seek out your positions within search engines. "This is a basic opportunity that many people are still missing out on," Charest says.

Open dialogue about your workplace with social marketing: As we explored earlier in Chapter 5, "Keeping Your Funnel Full," emerging social marketing tools—from public sites such as Facebook to employee-only locations such as McDonald's Station M—come with a double-edged sword that you need to gauge before jumping in. "We're still just at the start of social networking and what that means for recruiting," TMP's Charest says.

Social networking initiatives such as creating your corporate avatar—your online clone in a virtual reality—on Second Life might sound cool, she adds, but not if that sense of adventure doesn't match your workplace reality and employment brand. Don't jump in until you've done your research about whom the site is targeting and the type of information that is being shared.

Remember, when you get to the stage where you're considering the solicitation of user-generated content, the risk remains that you can't fully control what other people are saying about your company.

Learn more about user-generated content in Chapter 5, Keeping Your Funnel Full.

However, the right site might deliver just what you want. For example, LinkedIn.com—a social marketing site founded in 2003 to connect salaried workers—now counts 27 million members, representing all Fortune 500 companies and 150 different industries.[iv] The site specifically links workers with their peers, whether to network for new jobs or pursue new clients and business opportunities.

Show your hip factor by getting your job ads out on the street: Do you think your company is truly a leading-edge, hip technology user? Today's young hourly workers are, so get yourself right into their space. Mobile technology can deliver your job openings—from basic job descriptions to online applications—right to job seekers' cell phones and mobile devices. In practice, that means you can enable job seekers to see your available jobs when they walk by your storefront, subscribe to mobile job alerts—or even better—apply to jobs directly from their phones. These tactics truly enable you to create an in-the-moment connection with job seekers that is as relevant as the "Help Wanted" sign.

 ## Listen to job seekers.

Who are the silent experts when it comes to looking for an hourly job? Your candidates—and many businesses don't make the effort to learn what they have to say. Whether they ultimately become your employees, these people should be given a voice in telling you what works about your recruitment strategy. They also can share good insights about their experiences with your competitors.

As with all information, the most important thing as you collect this kind of market intelligence from your candidates is to act on appropriate suggestions. And do so with transparency. If, say, your candidates repeatedly tell you they want more opportunities to interact with their workplace peers, draw out how you're fixing this void in great detail. Tell them what you're going to do. Then do it. Finally, remind them exactly what you've done to address their concerns. It sounds simple, but it works.

Recruiting is a never-ending part of business. But it doesn't have to be all work.

As your business evolves, make sure you are investing in the right technological tools and developing repeatable processes that enable you to focus on your people—not the paperwork (even as you move more and more of that online). Computer applications and online capabilities offer streamlined ways to conduct core HR transactions, including background screenings, worker eligibility requirements and related tasks.

Your responsibility is to make sure your recruitment team is not just looking at the open jobs on the table but thinking strategically about ways to fuel your business with a constant pipeline of qualified candidates. Your people are your competitive advantage, so your recruitment strategy needs to be designed to drive the long-term success of your business.

Starbucks: Taking It to the Next Level

OPPORTUNITY: There were several recruiting challenges facing Phil Hendrickson, manager of global talent sourcing for Starbucks, in the fall of 2007, and he set out to address them in a strategic and rigorous manner. Starbucks was spending money on recruiting services and could not show a return on investment for these expenditures; there was a lot of recruiting activity but they could not measure its effectiveness; and the recruiting activity had no framework or process. Their recruiters were talented professionals who needed the tools and training necessary to stay on top of their game and there was a compelling interest in improving the experience of people applying to jobs on the corporate website.

SOLUTION: Hendrickson noted, "There were not sufficient resources (job boards, resume licenses, professional and association lists and free & innovative services) for recruiters to use. In the absence of these tools recruiters sometimes created ad hoc vendor relationships, or made redundant purchases for services that were not integrated through systems or governed within a process. Money was not effectively spent. "We increased the number of integrated job boards from 2 to more than 40 in four countries, diversifying their selection across industries and geographies so that their use could be targeted by skill, industry designation or candidate segment. We integrated boards from marketing to accounting to retail, as well as those targeting diverse segments within these specialties. We ensured compliance obligations were met through a suite of board relationships and we rolled out free and innovative services. These boards were integrated with our ATS, affording many advantages. They could be used quickly and easily, saving hundreds of manual-posting hours for recruiters so they could spend their time in more valuable activities. We could track the candidate responses, from view to apply, and we could measure the effectiveness of each. In addition, we could manage all of these boards from a single location and make available to recruiters, at the moment of posting, important information like the costs associated with the board, the remaining inventory on that board or the other sites that were already engaged." Starbucks expanded their sourcing tools with a selection of resume licenses, associations and other databases. They also opened direct channels into the military and mature worker candidate segment though media relationships and by earning an age-friendly certification.

> "We increased the number of integrated job boards from 2 to more than 40 in four countries."

RESULTS: Within this tools-rich environment Starbucks was able to drive down costs, eliminate redundancies and wasted recruiter activity, and were able to reach a broader selection of talent faster and often at no cost.

From the corner store to the corner office: measuring results and advanced recruiting techniques

Start by ensuring you have a solid analytical framework for assessing your recruitment strategy, including tracking the key data that will help you study the metrics that mean most to your business. You also need to ensure that new recruitment tools, such as a Talent Management System, are designed to help you streamline the basic transactions and reporting requirements for your business—and are scalable to grow with your employee volume.

Step back to look at your full employment practice. Are you maximizing your current resources—whether getting your real workplace story out on your corporate website or improving core repeatable processes? Your company is probably on a growth curve, so this might be the right time to update your Employment Value Proposition to reflect who you are and where you're going to get the right people on board.

Are you keeping your eyes on the horizon for emerging technology or resources? Talented people gravitate to talented companies, so explore whether hip new tactics such as social networking will further differentiate your company. Given the size of your business, make sure you are breaking down employment data to get valued data out to your regions, which will refine and improve local hiring.

Do new tactics pass the goal gut-check?

Social networking sounds edgy. Adding video to job descriptions would really be riding the technology wave. But are these tactics right for you? It's easy to get caught up in the latest trend or marketing fad, but it's important to make these tactics will truly benefit your bottom line. The following flowchart can serve as a gut-check for assessing new marketing tactics. And while you saw this earlier in the chapter, here I'm asking that you process it in reverse order, starting with the tactic you want to introduce and seeing if it connects to your business objective.

Tactic: What new action are you looking to try?

Strategy: How does this new tactic mesh and complement the other weapons in your arsenal?

Goal: How is your big picture impacted by the addition of this tactic?

Objective: Will you be able to achieve your primary business objective better now?

If you find you're able to connect the new tactic to your objective, the next step is to go back and ensure you have a sound metric for measuring its success.

Metric: Indicate specifically how you'll track the success of this new tactic.

Understand your recruiting costs

BEFORE	Hourly Recruitment Strategy			
	10 employees	**100 employees**	**1,000 employees**	**10,000 employees**
Frontline sales impact of inferior frontline workforce	80% frontline efficiency x $100,000 potential revenues $20,000 loss	80% frontline efficiency x $1M potential revenues $200,000 loss	80% frontline efficiency x $10M potential revenues $2M loss	80% frontline efficiency x $100M potential revenues $20M loss
Manager's time spent recruiting (at $20 hourly rate)	100 hours x $20/hr $2,000	1000 hours x $20/hr $20,000	10,000 hours x $20/hr $200,000	100,000 hours x $20/hr $2M
Newspaper ad costs (30 days)	$1,800 x 12 months $21,600	$4,500 x 12 months $54,000	$11,250 x 12 months $135,000	$28,125 x 12 months $337,500
Total frontline recruitment cost	$20,000 loss + $2,000 time + $21,600 ad cost **$43,600**	$200,000 loss + $20,000 time + $54,000 ad cost **$274,000**	$2M loss + $200,000 time + $135,000 ad cost **$2,335,000**	$20M loss + $2M time + $337,500 ad cost **$22,337,500**

AFTER — Hourly Recruitment Strategy

	10 employees	100 employees	1,000 employees	10,000 employees
Frontline sales impact of superior frontline workforce	100% frontline efficiency x $100,000 potential revenues ——— $0 loss	100% frontline efficiency x $1M potential revenues ——— $0 loss	100% frontline efficiency x $10M potential revenues ——— $0 loss	100% frontline efficiency x $100M potential revenues ——— $0 loss
Manager's time spent recruiting (at $20 hourly rate)	50 hours x $20/hr ——— $1,000	500 hours x $20/hr ——— $10,000	5,000 hours x $20/hr ——— $100,000	50,000 hours x $20/hr ——— $1M
Online job postings (30 days)	$150 posting fee x 5 postings ——— $750	$130 bulk rate x 50 postings ——— $6,500	$80 bulk rate x 240 postings ——— $19,200	$50 bulk rate x 2,400 postings ——— $120,000
Total frontline recruitment cost	$0 loss + $1,000 time + $750 ad cost ——— **$1,750**	$0 loss + $10,000 time + $6,500 ad cost ——— **$16,500**	$0 loss + $100,000 time + $19,200 ad cost ——— **$119,200**	$0 loss + $1M time + $120,000 ad cost ——— **$1,120,000**
Potential Savings	**96%**	**94%**	**95%**	**95%**

We wanted to keep this savings chart relatively simple, but if you really want to flesh this formula out, you can add even more metrics key to your business, such as time to hire, overtime paid, retention rate and WOTC compliance.

Sources

I   Kronos Talent Management. "Close the Loop: Improving Business Results Through Analytics." Talent Management Newsletter. November 2007.

II   Borrell Associates.

III Borrell Associates.

IV LinkedIn.com.

Notes